SEX AND THE CIVIL WAR

The Steven and Janice Brose Lectures in the Civil War Era

William A. Blair, editor

The Steven and Janice Brose Lectures in the Civil War Era are published by the University of North Carolina Press in association with the George and Ann Richards Civil War Era Center at Penn State University. The series features books based on public lectures by a distinguished scholar, delivered over a three-day period each fall, as well as edited volumes developed from public symposia. These books chart new directions for research in the field and offer scholars and general readers fresh perspectives on the Civil War era.

SEX AND THE CIVIL WAR

Soldiers, Pornography, and the
Making of American Morality

JUDITH GIESBERG

THE UNIVERSITY OF NORTH CAROLINA PRESS

Chapel Hill

© 2017 The University of North Carolina Press

All rights reserved

Designed by Jamison Cockerham
Set in Arno, designed by Robert Slimbach; Church in the Wildwood, by Beth Rufener; and Type No. 1, by Walden Font Co.
Typeset by Tseng Information Systems, Inc.

Cover illustration: *Le Boudoir*, postcard from the author's collection.

Library of Congress Cataloging-in-Publication Data
Names: Giesberg, Judith Ann, 1966– author.
Title: Sex and the Civil War : soldiers, pornography, and the making of American morality / Judith Giesberg.
Other titles: Steven and Janice Brose lectures in the Civil War era.
Description: Chapel Hill : The University of North Carolina Press, [2017] | Series: The Steven and Janice Brose lectures in the Civil War era | Includes bibliographical references and index.
Identifiers: LCCN 2016020978 | ISBN 9781469631271 (cloth : alk. paper) | ISBN 9781469652078 (pbk. : alk. paper) | ISBN 9781469631288 (ebook)
Subjects: LCSH: Pornography—Social aspects—United States—History—19th century. | Pornography—Moral and ethical aspects—United States—History—19th century. | Pornography—Law and legislation—United States—History—19th century. | Obscenity (Law)—United States—History—19th century. | Social norms—United States—History—19th century. | Sexual ethics—United States—History—19th century. | Sex—Social aspects—United States—History—19th century. | United States—History—Civil War, 1861–1865—Social aspects. | United States—History—Civil War, 1861–1865—Psychological aspects. | Vice control—United States—History—19th century.
Classification: LCC HQ472.U6 G54 2017 | DDC 306.77097309/034—dc23
LC record available at https://lccn.loc.gov/2016020978

*To Diego and Pablo,
who will hate that their mother dedicated
a book about porn to them*

CONTENTS

Acknowledgments xi

Introduction *1*

1 Lewd, Wicked, Scandalous:
American Pornography Comes of Age *12*

2 Storming the Enemy's Breastworks:
Civil War Courts-Martial and the Sexual
Culture of the U.S. Army Camp *33*

3 True Courage: Anthony Comstock and the
Crisis of the War *59*

4 Outraged Manhood of Our Age:
The Postwar Antipornography Campaign *82*

Epilogue *104*

Notes *109*

Bibliography *125*

Index *133*

FIGURES

1. "Catalogue of Popular Books" featuring works by George Thompson, 1859   *18*

2. Erotica dealer circular   *20*

3. Circular by erotica dealer Thomas Ormsby, 1861   *21*

4. "Interior of Railroad Car," *Frank Leslie's Magazine*, 1888   *24*

5. Edward Clay, "Amalgamation Waltz," 1839   *30*

6. Illustrations from *Fanny Hill*, 1830   *35*

7. Illustration from *The Life and Adventures of Cicily Martin*, 1846   *39*

8. "Ellen Jewett," lithograph by New York printer Henry R. Robinson, 1836   *43*

9. Cartes de visite from Thomas Lowry, *Story the Soldiers Wouldn't Tell*   *44*

10. Carte de visite of unknown Union soldier   *46*

11. Soldiers posing for photograph together   *47*

12. Soldiers posing for photograph with one's arm draped over the other's shoulders   *48*

13	Soldiers posing for choreographed photograph	49
14	Fashion plates, *Godey's Lady's Book*	50
15	Edwin Forbes, "The Showman in Camp," *Frank Leslie's Illustrated*, 1864	55
16	"How High Is Dis," stereoscopic photograph	56
17	Seventeenth Connecticut Monument, Gettysburg	60
18	"The Modern News Stand and Its Results," from Anthony Comstock, *Traps for the Young*, 1883	78
19	Stanhope miniatures	96
20	Cartoon lampooning Anthony Comstock, *The Masses*, 1915	99

ACKNOWLEDGMENTS

This project began with William A. Blair's invitation to deliver a series of lectures on pornography for the Steven and Janice Brose Lectures in the Civil War Era at the Pennsylvania State University. Bill nudged me in this direction, even though he preferred to talk about the topic in euphemism. Thank you to Steve and Jan for endowing a lecture series that has produced a line of distinguished books that breathe new life into the study of the period and for their interest and encouragement. At Penn State, too, I would like to thank faculty and graduate students who attended the lectures, asked probing questions, and offered excellent advice, particularly Amy Greenberg, Chris Hayashida-Knight, Matt Isham, Anthony Kaye, Ari Kelman, Anne Rose, Evan Rothera, Robert Sandow, Emily Seitz-Moore, and Sean Trainor. In my experience, Civil War historians are an incredibly generous and gregarious lot, always ready to share ideas, read one another's work, and provide feedback; Stephen Berry, Catherine Clinton, Lorien Foote, Matt Gallman, and Lesley Gordon read the manuscript carefully, corrected errors, and encouraged me to say more. Katie Jorgensen Gray managed to get through an early draft, even though this is not her period, and offered good advice. Bill Blair and Nina Silber read multiple drafts and pushed me to capture the big picture—if I have managed to do so, it is because of them. Paul Steege and Seth Koven talked things through with me at the beginning and the end. I am very fortunate to do what I do, where I do, and with such fantastic colleagues.

I was privileged to work again with the staff at the University of North Carolina Press, particularly Mark Simpson-Vos, Jay Mazzocchi, and Trish Watson; Trish's careful editing corrected many mistakes and protected me from much embarrassment. Archivists at Princeton University, the Library of Congress, and at the National Archives helped, even when they did not have anything to offer. Special thanks to Shawn Wilson and Catherine Johnson-Roehr at the Kinsey Institute for Research in Sex, Gender, and Reproduction at Indiana University, who guided me through the institute's rich collections, and Kenneth R. Cobb at the New York City Department of Records and Information Services for lending arrest and trial records. Thank you to the staff at the American Antiquarian Society who helped me during a research trip and follow-up inquiries. Eri Mizukane at the University of Pennsylvania's Van Pelt Library helped to track down images. Thank you to Villanova librarians Michael Foight and Jutta Seibert; Michael was on the lookout for materials for this project, checking eBay and rare book auctions, since the beginning. Thomas Lowry granted me access to his court-martial records database and agreed to let me use images from his own collection. Jami Arsenich helped in a bunch of ways and always when she had a million other things to do. Thank you to graduate students Rebecca Capobianco, Daniel Gorman Jr., Michael Johnson, James Kopaczewski, Michael Fischer, Kenneth Wohl, and Michaela Smith for their research assistance and careful and critical reading. I learned a great deal from each and am deeply proud of them. This project received welcome support from Villanova's University Summer Grant Program. I am grateful to Villanova's Subventions Committee for providing funds for illustrations. Thank you to Marc Gallicchio for arranging an early and well-timed sabbatical and for being a champion of his colleagues' work, and to Dean Jean Ann Linney for authorizing my leave.

My biggest thanks go to Ed, Diego, Pablo, and Marisol, who periodically live with absences, physical and mental, and who inspire me every day and in every way. I struggle to find words to express my gratitude to Ed for supporting, encouraging, and listening to me talk about this Civil War project or that one and all with more patience and good humor than seems fair to ask of anyone. Thank you, Ed, for teaching me everything I know about living and loving.

SEX AND THE CIVIL WAR

INTRODUCTION

In February 1865, Sherman's troops were making their way through the Carolinas, and Grant's forces were entrenched outside Petersburg—today we might declare the war all but won for the Union. But it certainly wasn't for those involved: the Confederacy, although its army was bleeding deserters, still had a few tricks up its sleeve, including sending delegates to Hampton Roads in an attempt to negotiate a ceasefire and endorsing a late plan to arm slaves. While the Confederate Congress was debating the controversial measure, the U.S. Congress discussed a matter that caught the attention of few and that barely registered in the congressional records: a law to protect soldiers from pornographic materials. The proposed act, part of Senate Bill 390, titled "An Act Relating to the Postal Laws," was part of an ongoing effort to manage the delivery of mail in the loyal states and prevent spies and other disloyal civilians from using the mail to pass on subversive materials.[1] In defense of the section on pornographic materials, Vermont senator Jacob Collamer insisted that the U.S. Postal Service had become "the vehicle for the conveyance of great numbers and quantities of obscene books and pictures, which are sent to the Army, and sent here and there and everywhere, and that it is getting to be a great evil."[2] There was some debate about details, but no senator quibbled with the basic premise of the act: that U.S. army soldiers needed to be protected from the ill effects of pornography and that it was Congress's responsibility to do so.[3]

None of the debate was concerned with what congressmen meant by "obscene books and pictures"—like the saying "I know it when I see it," lawmakers evinced a comfortable familiarity with what constituted pornography, and all accepted that it was hurting the Union war effort.[4] The law passed, providing for a fine of $500 to be levied against any person who knowingly mailed "an obscene book, pamphlet, picture print, or other publication."[5]

Although intended as a means of protecting Union soldiers and helping to secure victory, the first recorded arrest under the new measure was made in New York City in May 1865, when James Gayler, special agent to the Post Office, arrested Benjamin H. Day for "mailing obscene pictures."[6] Benjamin Henry Day was publisher of the *New York Sun*, one of the city's penny papers that enjoyed wide readership for its coverage of crimes and other topics that opened these papers up to charges of obscenity.[7] Day was released after posting bail. Eight more men were arrested under the federal measure between 1865 and the first three months of 1872: four in Chicago, one each in Wadsworth, Ohio, and Lansing, Michigan, and two additional arrests in New York, totaling nine arrests in seven years. In one case, the defendant was sentenced to a one-year prison term—exceeding the parameters of the federal measure—but in the other cases the accused was fined or the case never made it to court.[8] Either the obscene materials that had agitated federal lawmakers in the midst of the war were not making their way into the mails, or local enforcement was lackluster.

By contrast, in the next ten months, thirteen men and two women were arrested under similar charges, nearly all of them in New York and nearly all a result of the efforts of one man. Anthony Comstock, it is often said, burst onto the scene in 1872, one year after New York passed a strict antiobscenity law, and within months was given virtually unlimited authority under federal law to police the nation's morals by controlling not only what got into the mails but also what people wrote about sex and what they did. Two years before his death, reflecting on a lifetime of tireless efforts, in an interview to a

New York paper Comstock tried to quantify his efforts: "In the forty-one years I have been here, I have convicted persons enough to fill a passenger train of sixty-one coaches, sixty coaches containing sixty passengers each and the sixty-first almost full. I have destroyed 160 tons of obscene literature."[9] But what Comstock saw as victory over vice — train cars full of contrite pornographers and mail bags spilling over with yellow-covered books — might just as well be read as the triumph of pornography. While Comstock failed to eradicate porn, the federal and state laws named after him drove abortions underground, as women and men who performed them were arrested. At the same time these laws restricted women's access to information about how to safely avoid unwanted pregnancies. Indeed, by one scholar's estimate, "between 1872 and 1880, Comstock and his associates aided in the indictment of 55 persons whom Comstock identified as abortionists."[10] Intended to drive irregular medical practitioners out of business, the 1873 federal law, combined with physician-inspired and Republican-sponsored state laws restricting or outlawing abortion, inserted the state into matters that under common law had been private. Once in the law, these war-born measures stayed put — for nearly a century in some cases.

But wait, *what?* How did this whole thing happen? How did a measure sponsored by abolitionist congressmen to protect soldiers and to secure victory on the battlefield become the vehicle for an expansive effort to take control of women's reproduction? What connects this Civil War story with the battle waged, one hundred years later, by feminist lawyers that resulted in the landmark decision in *Roe v. Wade*? How did an effort to restrain men's sexual imagination give birth to an effort that controlled women's sexuality?

The story begins with the Young Men's Christian Association (YMCA). A group of concerned New York City businessmen and ministers, inspired by similar efforts in London, launched the YMCA in 1852, out of concern for the growing number of young male clerks who came to work in the city, where they were tempted by alcohol, prostitutes, and a wide variety of printed erotica sold on the street.

The YMCA offered clerks a library and lounge, equipped with wholesome reading materials, where they could spend their leisure hours and avoid the temptations of city life. When the Civil War began and many of these same clerks mustered in with the city's first regiments in May 1861, the YMCA sent them off stocked with hymnals and bibles. Board members created the Army Committee of the New York YMCA, which became the U.S. Christian Commission. USCC chaplains enlisted with the men, reporting back to the New York offices on their efforts to turn the U.S. Army into a new field of evangelical work.[11] They had their work cut out for them. Whereas some chaplains reported, as did J. W. Waldron, Thirty-First Regiment, New York Volunteer, that there was "a marked improvement in the conduct of our men since leaving New York," most complained that in camp "profanity and other wickedness vastly abounds."[12] Concerned to combat all sorts of immoral behavior, the USCC remained particularly interested in reading. In 1863 USCC chaplain J. C. Thomas, Eighty-Eighth Regiment, Illinois Volunteers, created a portable library system that supplied camps and hospitals with boxes full of carefully selected books intended as wholesome alternatives to the novels and other printed works circulated in camp. By 1865 some four hundred of these libraries were in circulation, mailed to soldiers in specially designed boxes and delivered at a discount by the railroads.[13] But the USCC still did not rest: in January 1865 it looked to friends in Congress to support a bill that would fight porn from the other end—from the point of entry into U.S. mailbags and railroad cars headed to soldiers in camp.

This was the beginning. Censorship of the federal mail became a powerful tool in the hands of reformers and others who used it against dealers in erotica, free love activists, birth control advocates, and abortion providers. States expanded the reach of the federal law by passing measures that criminalized the possession of "obscene" items. In the absence of a definition of "obscene," these laws worked to effectively silence political critics, feminists, and gay rights activists, until a series of twentieth-century court cases expanded First

Amendment speech protections to most previously outlawed expressions, with the exception of those that, applying "contemporary community standards," portray sex in "a patently offensive way" and that are wholly lacking in "serious literary, artistic, political, or scientific value."[14] The more expansive protections extended to all sorts of sexual expression today are dependent on how judges and others interpret "community standards," how contemporaries weigh free expression over protection from harm, and who needs the state's protection. In practice today, federal authorities have been reluctant to weigh in on such matters, with the exception of a number of recent initiatives intended to protect children from explicit materials on the Internet. That these initiatives have failed is no cause for celebration, but the situation highlights the entangled histories of sexuality, gender, and childhood. This should turn historians' attention to discovering the Civil War origins of a federal conversation about sex and sexual regulation, protecting the fighting men, and saving the nation for whom they fought.[15] This book is interested in discovering the Civil War origins of American antipornography. It asks big questions and provides only partial answers. Why, in the midst of the Civil War, did U.S. lawmakers settle on porn as a threat to men's morals and their bodies, rather than, well, the war? Although Americans took inspiration from European reformers when they spoke of protecting "youth" or "the young person" from obscene publications, why did only American reformers come to see young men, rather than men *and* women, as in need of protection? And what might an exploration of pornography and antipornography reveal about midcentury gender relations and the crisis of the Civil War?

A number of years ago historians began to ask if it might be useful to think of the Civil War as crisis in gender. The collapse of slavery threw gender identity in the South into disarray, one line of argument goes, dissolving the antebellum race and gender order and leaving a confusing set of expectations in its place, particularly for the (white) men who lost.[16] Victory was consequential to male gender identity, another study finds, as northern commentators celebrated the region's invigorated manhood, concluding, in essence, that the "manlier men had won the contest."[17] Others have shown how manhood was deeply contested within the ranks, with fissures developing between men who saw military service as confirming their calls for restraint and those who saw the war as an endorsement of male aggression.[18] That manhood was a disputed notion among the belligerents as much as if not more than between them now seems an established fact. Taking sex as its subject, this study looks at questions of manhood and masculinity with fresh eyes.

This book's central claim is that paying attention to the Civil War origins of antipornography offers us two dividends. First, by exploring soldiers' expanded access to and interactions with obscene materials, we can begin to understand the sexual culture of the camps. We long ago stopped buying the idea that Victorians were somehow less attuned to sex than modern Americans, but with the exception of discovering the earthiness of sexual expression in their letters home to wives and following rare references to prostitutes and prostitution, we know little about the sexual lives of soldiers.[19] Although for Civil War Americans sex was part of how they defined themselves as men, those of us who study the period have tended to look for it only in the narrowest possible terms when women were in the picture. But women also entered the camp, *as pictures*, and so too did men experience sex around—perhaps even with—other men. Taking sex and pornography seriously, it seems to me, will bring us closer to understanding the lived experiences of a generation of men.

Second, understanding the legislative reaction to pornography sheds light on how a victorious, resurgent nation-state sought to assert its moral authority first, of course, through emancipation but then also by redefining human relations of the most intimate sort, including sex and reproduction. That this latter tendency has remained stubbornly lodged in the state, reemerging in the form of pronatalist policies that have followed all of America's subsequent wars, suggests that we have overlooked an important legacy of the Civil War. Rather than producing a permanent renegotiation of relations of gender and power, war, Susan Jeffords has argued, "enables gender relations to survive, offering territory in which to adjust, test, and reformulate general social relations."[20] Win or lose, the American nation-state emerges from wars morally regenerated and, rather than accepting a new gender reality, sets about adjusting the old one to a new set of circumstances. The U.S. Civil War produced a crisis in gender, as all wars do, in shaking up the ground on which antebellum understandings of manhood and womanhood stood, but postwar adjustments ensured that power relations between women and men did not change. Indeed, if there is one thing we can learn from exploring the intertwined history of porn, antiporn, and anti–birth control/abortion, it is that war does more to sustain gender hierarchy than to upset it.

I bought Thomas P. Lowry's 1994 book, *The Story the Soldiers Wouldn't Tell: Sex in the Civil War*, in my first year of graduate school. Like other books that came out in the late 1980s and early 1990s—Debra Grey White's *Aren't I a Woman*, Nina Silber and Catherine Clinton's *Divided Houses*, and Elizabeth Leonard's *Yankee Women*, for example—Lowry's book seemed to hold promise for helping us to understand gender in the war. I eagerly read them all as I began to think about Civil War history as a field of gender inquiry. Unlike the first generation of scholarly books that brought gender analysis to bear on the Civil War, though—and that, by implication, made it safe for women to enter the field—Lowry's book was intended for a popular audience whose members were not interested in how social and gender historians were changing the historiography. Male readers of *The Story the Soldiers Wouldn't Tell* could be expected to chortle at the author's opening lines—"There was no sex during the Civil War. Everyone knows it."[21]—and then follow the author, with a wink and a nudge, through chapters on prostitutes, pornography, masturbation, homosexuality, and contraception. Intended as a lively romp through the sexual theater of the Civil War, the book made no attempt to situate these stories within the contemporary context, analyze critically the subject matter, or weigh in on the meaning of all the rich material that the author found. A striking feature of the book is the middle section of illustrations, an odd mixture of soldiers suffering from the late stages of syphilis and of erotic cartes de visite featuring close-up pictures of nude women. The book has been a commercial success, of course,[22] but scholars have stayed away from the book: instead of illuminating the experience of sex in the Civil War, of somehow making wartime women and men more understandable to modern Americans, the book feeds readers' already insatiable desire for all things Civil War. It can make us "love" the war, to paraphrase Drew Faust, in all its spectacular violence, even more by adding sex to it.[23] Civil War Americans, readers of Lowry's book concluded, were gloriously free of "Victorian" prudishness, so what should stop us from indulging?[24] Why not, George Costanza once asked in an episode of *Seinfeld*, have sex *and* eat a sandwich?

Except finding evidence of Civil War pornography is not the same thing as learning that "they were just like us"—or "we should be more like them"—as Lowry's readers would have it. Indeed, some Civil War Americans became profoundly concerned about the war's mixing of sex and violence and sponsored a series of measures to disentangle the two. Trained in the history of gender, my interests have always been in uncovering the experiences of women in this period. Yet, there are few women in the pages that follow, and those that are here are mostly imaginary—women are represented in cartes de visite, adorn the backs of playing cards, await our gaze at the end of a stereoscope, or appear as crude sketches in erotic fiction. "War," Margaret Higonnet, Jane Jenson, Sonya Michel, and Margaret Collins Weitz explained, "must be understood as a *gendering* activity, one that ritually marks the gender of all members of society."[25] Although women appeared in camp as cooks, laundresses, nurses, soldiers in disguise, prostitutes, and visiting wives, soldiering marked one as a man. Indeed, this was the case even when some of those soldiers turned out to be women.[26] Men noted women's flesh-and-blood presence in camp because it reminded them of home, but doing so marked women as outsiders. Erotic images and stories about imaginary women also marked women as outside the experience of soldiering. The images of women that adorned *The Story the Soldiers Wouldn't Tell* functioned in a similar way, it seemed to me: they marked the Civil War as male terrain at the precise moment when female scholars were discovering it. So, I determined that someday I would go back to Lowry's book, because I suspected that there was more to be said about the subject. I chose the title for this book, *Sex and the Civil War*, because what follows offers some answers to the questions that book raised for me.

The chapters that follow explore the U.S. government's antipornography campaign and those who resisted it, in hopes that doing so will allow us to better understand the sexual culture of the era, how Civil War Americans interacted with it, and some of the long-term ramifications of the battle over Civil War pornography. The chapters are organized chronologically, with the first describing the antebellum production of pornography and transatlantic attempts to control its circulation, the second considering wartime consumption, the third chapter examining Anthony Comstock's military experience in the war, and the fourth assessing the wartime and postwar antipornography measures.

Chapter 1 places the Civil War in the context of growing concern about and expanding access to erotic publications, in the United States, France, and Great Britain. It argues that the particular timing of and circumstances surrounding the U.S. Civil War paved the way for the emergence and wide distribution of domestically produced pornography. Although erotic publications enjoyed wide distribution and officials from Boston to San Francisco expressed concern about the books and magazines, the industry was strongly associated with New York City, where a number of publishers produced the stuff and were first to exploit the opportunities opened up by delivery through the mail. This chapter examines New York officials' efforts to prosecute erotica dealers and considers how conventions of antislavery literature contributed to the emergence of an antebellum erotic imagination.

Chapter 2 follows the mailbags delivered to the front lines, and, through an examination of court-martial records and regimental order books, it locates erotic items in camp, explores their circulation, and considers U.S. military policy with regard to erotica. Whenever possible, this chapter describes the content of these works and seeks to understand how men in camp interacted with it. Readers will note that this chapter includes a discussion of a wide variety of published works, including popular songs and magazines, that were not produced with erotic intent but that were reimagined and repurposed in the all-male milieu of the U.S. Army camp. Whether such items fit properly in a study of pornography remains an open question; I include them here because they form part of a constellation of images of women displayed or circulated in camp with the intention of appealing to men's erotic imagination. In some circumstances, letters from and photographs of wives and sweethearts might also fit the description. I do not discuss them here because women produced these items for the personal use of the recipient and not for sale or widespread distribution. Readers might see this distinction as arbitrary or perhaps as a missed opportunity.

Anthony Comstock is the subject of chapter 3, because he provides the key link between a wartime concern about pornography and the postwar antipornography campaign. This chapter aims to understand how Comstock came to be concerned about protecting boys and young men from words, images, and thoughts that could make them violent and unmanly. Particularly vulnerable were boys and young men in all-male milieus, such as boarding schools or, in Comstock's own case, the military camp. Chapter 4 examines two federal antiporn measures—one passed in 1865 and a more expansive one passed in 1873 that became known as the Comstock Law—in their contexts and seeks to answer some of the remaining questions, such as how pornography, birth control, and abortion came to be associated in a cluster of laws reflecting postwar concerns about marriage and family.

All the evidence I examine here refers to the problem of pornography in the U.S. Army. That Confederate soldiers did not have access to this stuff or produce their own seems unlikely. Mary Elizabeth Massey noted the effects of the Confederacy's chronic paper shortage by describing widespread repurposing: "Every scrap of paper was forced into use—old letters, envelopes, fly-leaves of books, leaves of account books and note books, wrapping paper, old bills, and, late in the war, Confederate money."[27] When a Confederate version of *Fanny Hill* is identified in a collection, it will likely have been printed on wallpaper, like some southern newspapers were during the war.

ONE

LEWD, WICKED, SCANDALOUS

American Pornography Comes of Age

The wartime prohibition against pornography unfolded within a transatlantic context, as policy initiatives and criminal trials in Europe affected and shaped decisions in the United States and vice versa. The first federal attempt to control the trade in illicit publications came in the form of an inauspicious section of the 1842 U.S. customs law that outlawed the importation of these materials. Before 1842, only Vermont had passed an antipornography statute; perhaps this explains Vermont senator Jacob Collamer's enthusiastic support for the 1865 measure. Associating obscene materials with foreign imports has a particular American ring to it, but the 1842 law also reflected a reality on the ground — there seems to have been no domestically produced pornography until after imports were outlawed.[1] "America has made of late years great progress in the production of books . . . of an improper character," the enthusiastic bibliographer Henry Spencer Ashbee noted in his 1877 *Index Librorum Prohibitorum*, published under the nom de plume Pisanus Fraxi.[2] The year 1857 proved to be critical in the intercontinental trade in pornography; it was the year that French author Gustave Flaubert was tried and acquitted for his 1856 novel *Madame Bovary*, Parliament passed Lord Campbell's Obscene Publications Act, and U.S. lawmakers strengthened the 1842 customs law.[3] Britain's Campbell Act set important precedents. Initiated by antivice organizations whose members referred to obscene publications as a "deadly acid" comparable to "strychnine, or arsenic," the bill elicited fierce debate among lawmakers over the meaning of the term "obscene." Declaring classics and other items that might be found in "gentlemen's" collections off-limits, the Campbell Act defined as obscene materials specifically intended to "corrupt the morals of youth."[4] Focused on prosecution at the point of sale, the law exposed the class biases of its authors, "gentlemen" who might be proud collectors of "the classics" but who nonetheless "knew porn when they saw it." Completing the perfect storm, the word "pornography" appeared in the *Oxford English Dictionary* in 1842 as one of a number of "lower classes of art" and in 1857 as a "description of prostitutes or of prostitution."[5] By the time American lawmakers became concerned about the hazards of pornography during the U.S. Civil War, "a kind of galaxy of the most explicit pornographic writing was already in place in the minds of connoisseurs."[6]

Policy initiatives were driven by the friction and tension produced by decisions made elsewhere, as Americans and Europeans reacted to legislative efforts overseas. The Brits, for instance, were disgusted when New York customs agents seized and destroyed a catalog produced by the Royal Museum of Naples, pointing out that the American traveler from whom it had been confiscated paid $150–$200 for the item. In the midst of the heated debate over the Campbell Act, American antiporn enthusiasm threatened to blur the line between art and pornography and sully some of what separated a gentleman from the "lower classes."[7] Unlike in Britain and France, the inauspicious way in which antipornography measures were passed in the United States—buried in a customs law and tucked between rules for the proper use of the U.S. Mail—suggests that little public conversation accompanied these measures.

Well before Anthony Comstock, there was abundant evidence to suggest that prosecution did little to curtail the trade in obscene publications. In fact, the antebellum trade in pornography was nurtured in an environment of increased surveillance. In the decade before the war, new customs laws and periodic local commitments to stamping out vice helped establish preconditions for a wartime explosion of porn. Much of the antebellum story about porn played out among a group of erotica dealers in New York City.

Beyond this story is an unacknowledged back history involving the publishing activities of abolitionists. While condemning the cruelty of slavery, authors of abolitionist tracts expanded access to a variety of materials that included scenes of sex and violence. Intended to arouse contempt for the abusive and depraved sexual practices of slaveholders, humanitarian reformers were nonetheless acutely aware of how closely the literature they produced aligned with the unchecked urges they condemned, or how their readers might simply be aroused.[8] Antislavery authors worked consciously to avoid comparisons with pornography, and of course, abolitionist authors were never the subject of local prosecution. (Their sentiments were tapped, as we shall see in later chapters, by antipornography crusaders.) The explicit content of reformers' tracts and books muddled attempts to build a consensus about what constituted the obscene and, in so doing, helped pave the way for porn's triumph. This chapter tells both of these stories.

In December 1854, New York City police arrested Thomas Ormsby and John Atchison for selling obscene books at their shop on Nassau Street in Lower Manhattan in the center of New York's thriving printing and publishing trade. Seeking an indictment against the men in February, the district attorney described the two as "scandalous and evil disposed persons" who were "devising, contriving and intending the morals of the Youth as well as of other good citizens of the said State to corrupt and to raise and create in their minds, inordinate and lustful desires."[9] At their shop, police found "a trunk filled with certain lewd, wicked, scandalous, infamous, and obscene printed books, many in number and of divers titles." The district attorney read several titles into the proceedings, and several books were produced as evidence. These included *The Life and Adventures of Silas Shovewell*, *The Curtain Drawn Up, or the Education of Laura*, and *Fanny Hill, or Memoirs of a Woman of Pleasure*. *The Voluptuary, or Women's Witchery, a Romance of Passion*, however, was "so lewd, wicked and obscene, that the same would be offensive to the court and improper to be placed upon the records thereof." Concerned not to offend the sensitivities of the court, the district attorney expected them to take his word for it, but in any case, the vivid description of the shop and its contents likely were enough to implicate the two. If not, the district attorney produced a witness, James Twain, who admitted to having purchased from Atchison, at the same address, a book called *The Mysteries of Venus, or the Amatory Life and Adventures of Kitty Pry*. Under oath, the witness described the book as having "a tendency to demoralize being of a grossly obscene character."[10] Whether that book, too, was admitted into evidence is unclear, but in any case the jury indicted Atchison for "selling obscene books."[11] What became of Ormsby's indictment is unclear, but the charges against Atchison were dropped when Mayor Fernando Wood interceded on his behalf, promising that Atchison "will refrain from such practices hereafter and in consideration of his family."[12]

Three men indicted on similar charges in March were not as fortunate. Terence Morris, Arthur Crown, and John (perhaps Jeremiah) Farrell stood before a grand jury on March 12, and each pleaded guilty. According to the district attorney, Morris and Crown "expos[ed] and offer[ed] for sale and solicit[ed] purchasers for a certain printed book entitled *The Secret Habits of the Female Sex, Letters addressed to a mother on the Evils of Solitude and Its Seductive Temptations to Young Girls*, containing divers lewd, indecent and filthy pictures." Even more than the contents of the book, though, the prosecutor found the illustrated advertisements contained in the book to be "scandalous and indecent" and "offensive to the morals of youth and men and women." To make his point, the district attorney read the titles of the advertised books into the record. They included:

The Musical Student
The Story of a Rake
Adventures of a Bed Stead
Julia, or Where Is the Woman That Wouldn't

Venus in the Closet
Intrigues of Three Days
Memoirs of an Old Man of Twenty
The Intrigues and Secret Amours of Napoleon
Memoirs of a Woman of Pleasure on the Singular and
  Surprising Adventures of Thermidore and Rozette
Memoirs of a Man of Pleasure, or the Amours, Intrigues
  and Adventures of Sir Charles Manly

According to the district attorney, the "lewd, scandalous, and indecent" book that Farrell was caught selling was titled *Mysteries of Women, or Guide to the Unwary Containing Advice to Husbands and Wives, regarding the means of making the marriage bed the throne of Venus' Joys*. Like the long list of books named in the previous two indictments that day, *Mysteries* contained "divers lewd, indecent and filthy pictures" and illustrated advertisements.[13]

All four cases were heard before the 1857 customs law expanded the definition of "obscene materials," giving local law enforcement officials more leeway to pursue prosecutions against banned imports.[14] The cases emerged instead from local initiatives. Following the election of Democrat Fernando Wood, the new mayor answered critics who charged that he would be soft on crime by ordering the city's police force "to investigate and report all violations of morals laws."[15] The cluster of cases brought before grand juries in the late 1850s did little to deter sellers of erotica. In fact, local prosecutions helped to expand the market for and supply of pornography.[16]

Although lawmakers were wont to dismiss porn as a foreign import, entrepreneurs in Boston and New York responded to the new customs laws by stepping up domestic production, often by pirating European works but also by encouraging local authors, such as George Thompson, who was one of the period's most prolific American authors of erotica. Following the pattern set by Europeans, American authors assumed noms de plume; even here they unapologetically copied from one another. For instance, George Thompson's most evocative moniker was Paul de Kock (fig. 1), the pen name of a French author of popular sensationalist literature. These names served as code for readers, who came to expect particularly racy works from authors such as de Kock.

By the 1860s, several American wholesalers had built a successful network of domestically produced and distributed erotica.[17] In her dissertation on the trade, Elizabeth Haven Hawley identified American imprints for hundreds of erotic books, including *Mysteries of Venus*, the book John Atchison was charged with selling, and *Memoirs of a Woman of Pleasure, Memoirs of a Man of Pleasure*, and *Julia*, among others named in the 1855 indictments against Morris, Crown, and Farrell.[18] Covered in cheap yellow paper, American-produced erotic books were printed in Boston, New York, and Philadelphia and sold at newsstands, at railroad stations, and along docks.[19] Police might detain Atchison, Ormsby, Morris, Crown, or Farrell, but there were other men ready to take their places while they stood trial.

Indeed, Ormsby, Farrell, and, despite Mayor Wood's assurances, Atchison were back at work soon after their indictments. By the early 1860s all three were selling their goods in a burgeoning mail order marketplace they helped create. Because of changes in the postal code, after 1851 bound books were admitted into the U.S. Mail, opening up new possibilities for erotica manufacturers and sellers looking to avoid local prosecution at the point of sale and seeking to expand their clientele.[20] Entrepreneurs such as Boston's William Berry and New Yorker George Ackerman were the first to see the possibilities of mail order pornography.[21] As Donna Dennis has shown, Ackerman launched the first American "fancy paper," the weekly *Venus Miscellany*. During 1856–57 the paper enjoyed good circulation, offering subscribers four pages of illustrations, short stories, jokes, advertisements, and letters to the editor. A little less lowbrow, perhaps, than the yellow-covered books hawked on Nassau Street or the flash weeklies of the previous decade, Ackerman's *Venus Miscellany* featured letters from middle-class married women and men. Ackerman intended to sell the paper exclusively through the mail, and he

CATALOGUE OF

POPULAR BOOKS.

Attention is called to the following Catalogue of cheap Publications, just issued. These Books are got up different from anything of the kind ever offered to the public. They are all handsomely illustrated with Plates.

La Tour De Nesle; or, The Amours of Marguerite of Burgundy,	50
The Amours of a Quaker; or, The Voluptuary,	50
The Loves of Byron, his various Intrigues with Celebrated Women,	50
Charles the Second, Earl of Rochester, and Buckingham's Intrigues,	50
The Chevallier; a thrilling tale of Love and Passion,	50
Confessions of a Lady's Waiting Maid; or, The Veil Uplifted,	50
City Crimes; or, Life in New York and Boston,	50
Revenge, a Tale of deep, mysterious, and great Crimes,	50
Jack Harold, by Greenhorn, 16 Illustrations,	50
The Criminal; or, The Adventures of Jack Harold,	25
The Outlaw; or, The Felon's Fortunes, a Sequel to the Criminal,	25
The Road to Ruin; or, Felon's Doom—the end of the Series,	25
Aristotle, Illustrated,	50
Complete Masterpiece,	25
Isabel of Arragon, being Intrigues of the Court,	25
Adventures of a Sofa; or, Drawing-Room Intrigues,	25
Marie de Clairville; or, The Confessions of a Boarding School Miss,	25
Flora Montgomery; or, The Factory Girl's Adventures,	25
The Bridal Chamber and its Mysteries,	25
The Intrigues and Amours of Aaron Burr,	25
The Mysteries of Bond Street, fashionable dissipation,	25
Private Life of Lola Montez—enough said,	25
Harriet Wilson; or, a Woman of Pleasure,	25
Madeline, the Avenger; or, Seduction and its Consequences,	25
Paul, the Profligate; or, Paris as it is,	25
Adventures of a Country Girl; or, Gay scenes in my Life,	25
Venus in Boston, an exciting Tale of City Life,	25
The Adventures of a Libertine,	25
Evil Genius; or, The Spy of the Police,	25

Sharps and Flats; or, The Perils of City Life,	25
The Lame Devil; or, Asmodeus in Boston,	25
Demon of Gold; or, The Miser's Daughter,	25
Dashes of Life, by Our Ned,	25
The Wedding Night; or, Advice to Bridegrooms; plain, five plates,	25
The Wedding Night; or, Advice to Bridegrooms; colored, five plates,	38
Secret Passion; plain, five plates,	25
" " colored, five plates,	38
Ladies' Garter, Illustrated, By Greenhorn,	25
Fanny Greely; or, Confessions of a Free Love Sister,	25
The Gay Girls of New York, . . by Greenhorn,	25
Kate Castleton, the Beautiful Milliner,	25
Harry Glindon, the Man of Many Crimes,	25
Adolene, the Female Adventurer,	25
Julia Maxwell; or, The Mysteries of Brooklyn, by Greenhorn,	25
Alice Wade; or, The Seducer's Fearful Doom,	25
Asmodeus; or, The Iniquities of New York, by Greenhorn,	25
New York Life; or, Mysteries of Upper Tendom Revealed, by Greenhorn,	25
The Coquette of Chestnut Street,	25
The California Widow,	25
The Life of Kate Hastings,	25
The Charming Young Man. By P. De Kock,	25
Mysteries and Miseries of Philadelphia,	25
Art of Boxing, Without a Master. By Owen Swift,	13
The Secret Habits of the Female Sex, plain plates,	25
" " " " colored,	38
Venus in the Cloister, plain plates,	25
" " colored "	38
Marriage Bed, six plates, colored,	38
" " " plain,	25
Advice to Husbands and Wives, 4 plates, plain,	25
" " " " 4 plates, col'd,	38
Broussais, Self-Preservation, 6 plates, colored,	38
Tom Brown's Jest Book,	13
Female Policy Detected,	13

WORKS OF CHARLES PAUL DE KOCK.—Uniform Edition.

The Adventures of a Musical Student, Illustrated,	25
The Mysteries of Venus; or, Lessons of Love, "	25
The Amours of Lady Augusta Clayton, "	25
The History of a Rake, "	25
The Secret Amours of Napoleon, "	25
Don Pedro in Search of a Wife, "	25
The Bar Maid of the Old Point House, "	25
The Intrigues of Three Days, "	25
Tales of Twilight, "	25
The Child of Nature Improved by Chance, "	25
Julia; or, Where is the Woman that Wouldn't, "	25
The Adventures of a French Bedstead, "	25

Brother James; or, The Libertine. Illustrated,	25
Memoirs of a Woman of Pleasure, "	25
The Two Lovers; or, Fred in a Fix, "	50
Cerisette; or, the Amours of an Actress, "	25
Memoirs of an Old Man of Twenty-five, "	50
Memoirs of a Man of Pleasure, "	50
The Gay Grisettes, "	25
Melting Moments; or, Love among the Roses, "	25
Gustavus, the Don Juan of France, "	25
Venus' Album; or, Rosebuds of Love, "	50
Henry; or, Life of a Libertine, "	25
John, the Darling of the Ladies, "	25

WHOLESALE DEALERS MOST LIBERALLY DEALT WITH.

Fig. 1. Paul de Kock was the nom de plume of erotica author George Thompson. Noms de plume signaled to consumers the erotic content of the work. ("Catalogue of Popular Books," Oshea, 1859; courtesy American Antiquarian Society)

never advertised locally.[22] Preferring the wider reach of the sporting press, Ormsby and Atchison advertised their yellow-colored books and other paraphernalia in papers like the *New York Clipper*, which featured a steadily growing list of mail order erotica throughout the Civil War.

Newspaper advertisements and publisher's circulars are critical sources for understanding the antebellum trade in pornography (fig. 2), for, prohibited and pilfered or destroyed by those who confiscated them, the books and prints no longer exist. Indeed, Hawley found that many surviving books were missing illustrations, as pages had been ripped out and were separated from the originals. In one case, a collector rescued erotic engravings that had been dumped in the garbage by prosecutors in an 1850 case (the collection of prints was only recently donated to the American Antiquarian Society).[23] Erotica produced and consumed in the Civil War era that still exists remains primarily in the hands of private collectors; little has found its way into institutional collections. In her dissertation research Hawley relied on bibliographer Ashbee, whose 1877 *Index Librorum Prohibitorum* listed and described many books that have vanished; "ghosts in the historical record," she called them.[24]

Circulars offer historians some sense of what was available for U.S. army soldiers. Although charged three times for selling indecent books, Ormsby continued to operate in the open during the war. Calling his business "Thomas Ormsby's Commission Bureau and General Purchasing Agency," the bookseller hoped to lend his business an official air (fig. 3). Ormsby's circular offered all sorts of items for sale, including jewelry, guns, clothing, and erotica. The titles seem a little less racy than those read to the grand jury at his 1855 indictment, and some were thinly disguised as intended for physiological instruction: *Dictionary of Love*, for instance, which was described as "a remarkable Text-Book for all Loves, as well as a Complete Guide to Matrimony, and a Companion of Married Life." Or *Woman's Form; or, Female Beauties*, "Being a Complete Analysis and Description of

PRIVATE CIRCULAR, FOR GENTLEMEN ONLY. No. 2.

NEW BOOKS!

Superior to Fanny Hill, or any other Fancy Work ever Published!

EVERY PICTURE A "GEM!"

Beautiful, "Amorous," and Seductive, Drawn and Engraved expressly for the Books, by a French Artist. One Picture worth the price of the Book!

NOW READY,

THE ROUE'S POCKET COMPANION;

OR,

GEMS from VENUS' MISCELLANY.

The most Beautifully Written and Elegantly Illustrated "Fancy and Amorous Work" that has ever appeared in this country, containing 200 pages of reading, which is a perfect love feast, and 10 magnificent engravings, designed expressly for this Work, by one of the first French Artists.

PRICE, $3 00.

ALSO JUST READY,

THE FESTIVAL OF LOVE;

OR,

REVELS at the FOUNT of VENUS.

One of the most Exquisite, Fascinating, and Amorous Work of the age—and making a splendid companion to the "Gems;" translated from the Italian, and beautifully Illustrated with 12 Splendid Amorous Pictures, elegantly colored—the whole forming a work of rare beauty.

PRICE, $3 00.

Either of the above Works will be sent to any part of the United States or Canadas, post-paid, on receipt of the price; or parties wishing can have them sent by Express, which is more certain and safe—or by remitting 54 cents in addition to the price of the Book, they can be sent in a letter, sealed close from observation.

P. S.—Books packed in such a manner as to defy detection—and all letters confidential—enclose money carefully—send your address plainly written—and direct all letters same as the enclosed card.

PRIVATE CIRCULAR, FOR GENTLEMEN ONLY.

GENUINE FANCY BOOKS!

BEAUTIFULLY PRINTED! ELEGANTLY COLORED PLATES! HANDSOMELY BOUND!

Every work named on this Circular is printed from new type, on fine paper, handsomely illustrated with Beautiful Colored Plates, and richly bound in cloth. They can be sent either by Mail or Express, with perfect safety, and done up in such a manner as to defy detection.

Persons ordering can rest assured that their orders will be promptly and faithfully attended to.

EVERY WORK NAMED IS EXACTLY AS REPRESENTED.

FANNY HILL, Her Life and Amours, 10 colored plates, . . $2 00
ROSE DE AMOUR, The French Courtezan, 10 colored plates, . . 2 00
LUSTFUL TURK, or Love in the Harem, 10 colored plates, . . 2 00
TWO COUSINS, Their Confessions. 10 colored plates, . . 2 00
SILAS SHOVEWELL, His Amours with the Nuns, 10 colored plates. 2 00
CURTAIN DRAWN UP, or The Education of Laura, 10 colored plates. 2 00

VOLUPTUOUS CONFESSIONS IN BED, 5 colored plates, . . $1 00
MADAME CELESTINE, Her Intrigues, 5 colored plates, . . 1 00
CICILY MARTIN, The Woman of Pleasure, 5 colored plates, . . 1 00
CABINET OF VENUS UNLOCKED, 5 colored plates, . . 1 00
FLASH AND FRISKY SONGSTER, 5 colored plates, . . 1 00

FANNY HILL

LARGEST SIZE, 24 COLORED PLATES—THE LARGEST WORK EVER PRINTED OF THE KIND—IT IS A SPLENDID VOLUME, ... $5 00

FRENCH TRANSPARENT PLAYING CARDS. The finest article in the Fancy Style that has ever been produced—they can be played with the same as a common card by persons unacquainted with them—and by holding them to the light you have 52 BEAUTIFULLY Colored Fancy Pictures. Price, ... $2 00
FRENCH "SAFES," OR "CONDOMS," Warranted—The only system Preventive against Disease or Frequency. Manufactured from fine transparent India Rubber—they cover the Penis entire, and increase the pleasures. Price, single, 50 cts, one dozen, ... $3 00
PRINTS OF VARIOUS SIZES, ... From 50 cts. to $2 00 each.
TOBACCO BOXES, Double covers, illustrated, Price, ... $2 00
CIGAR CASES, 10 illustrations, secret drawer, ... 3 00

☞ Recollect, none of the above can be had at our office in New York. All orders must be sent by mail, and they will receive early and prompt attention, and the articles ordered forwarded to their destination, in the most compact, reliable and expeditious manner.

Fig. 2. Circulars list the titles of works, many of which no longer exist. *Fanny Hill* was a standard text offered by period erotica dealers. ("Private Circular no. 2," Genuine Fancy Books; courtesy American Antiquarian Society)

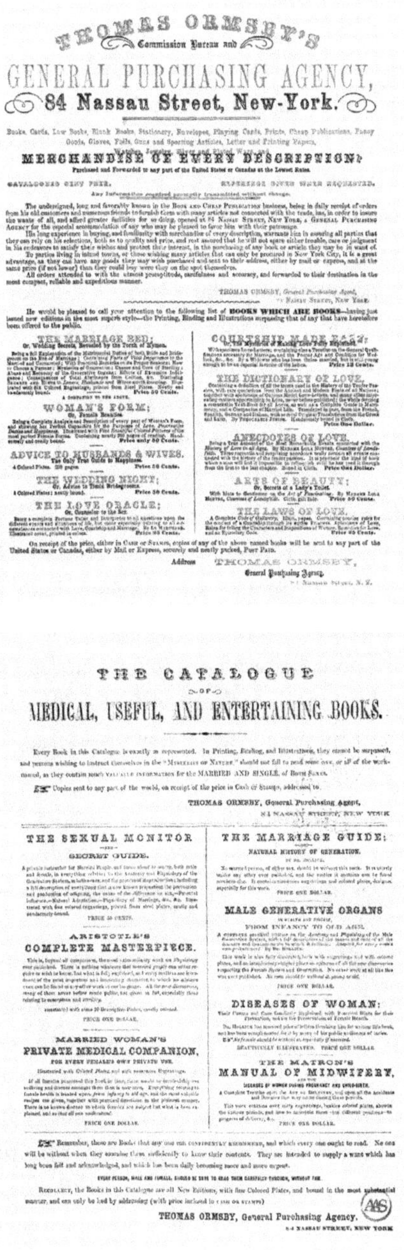
THOMAS ORMSBY'S
Commission Bureau and
GENERAL PURCHASING AGENCY,
84 Nassau Street, New-York.
Books, Cards, Law Books, Blank Books, Stationery, Envelopes, Playing Cards, Prints, Cheap Publications, Fancy Goods, Gloves, Foils, Guns and Sporting Articles, Letter and Printing Papers,
MERCHANDISE OF EVERY DESCRIPTION
Purchased and Forwarded to any part of the United States or Canadas at the Lowest Rates.
The undersigned, long and favorably known in the Book and Cheap Publication business, being in daily receipt of orders from his old customers and numerous friends to furnish them with many articles not connected with the trade, has, in order to insure the wants of all, and afford greater facilities for so doing, opened at 84 Nassau Street, New York, a General Purchasing Agency for the especial accommodation of any who may be pleased to favor him with their patronage.
His long experience in buying, and familiarity with merchandise of every description, warrants him in assuring all parties that they can rely on his selections, both as to quality and price, and rest assured that he will not spare either trouble, care or judgment in his endeavors to satisfy their wishes and protect their interest, in the purchasing of any book or article they may be in want of.
To parties living in inland towns, or those wishing many articles that can only be procured in New York City, it is a great advantage, as they can have any goods they may wish purchased and sent to their address, either by mail or express, and at the same price (if not lower) than they could buy were they on the spot themselves.
All orders attended to with the utmost promptitude, carefulness and accuracy, and forwarded to their destination in the most compact, reliable and expeditious manner.
THOMAS ORMSBY, General Purchasing Agent,
He would be pleased to call your attention to the following list of BOOKS WHICH ARE BOOKS—having just issued new editions in the most superb style—the Printing, Binding and Illustrations surpassing that of any that have heretofore been offered to the public.
THE MARRIAGE BED;
Or, Wedding Secrets, Revealed by the Torch of Hymen.
COURTSHIP MADE EASY;
THE DICTIONARY OF LOVE.
WOMAN'S FORM;
Or, Female Beauties.
ANECDOTES OF LOVE.
ADVICE TO HUSBANDS & WIVES.
ARTS OF BEAUTY;
Or, Secrets of a Lady's Toilet.
THE WEDDING NIGHT;
THE LOVE ORACLE;
THE LAWS OF LOVE.
THOMAS ORMSBY,
General Purchasing Agency.
THE CATALOGUE
OF
MEDICAL, USEFUL, AND ENTERTAINING BOOKS.
Every Book in this Catalogue is exactly as represented. In Printing, Binding, and Illustrations, they cannot be surpassed, and persons wishing to instruct themselves in the "Mysteries of Nature," should not fail to read some one, or all of the works named, as they contain much valuable information for the MARRIED AND SINGLE, of Both Sexes.
Copies sent to any part of the world, on receipt of the price in Cash or Stamps, addressed to
THOMAS ORMSBY, General Purchasing Agent,
THE SEXUAL MONITOR
AND
SECRET GUIDE.
THE MARRIAGE GUIDE;
NATURAL HISTORY OF GENERATION.
PRICE ONE DOLLAR.
MALE GENERATIVE ORGANS
ARISTOTLE'S
COMPLETE MASTERPIECE.
DISEASES OF WOMAN:
MARRIED WOMAN'S
PRIVATE MEDICAL COMPANION,
THE MATRON'S
MANUAL OF MIDWIFERY,
THOMAS ORMSBY, General Purchasing Agency.

Fig. 3. New York erotica dealer Thomas Ormsby faced local prosecution on three separate occasions before the Civil War. During the war he sold erotica by mail order advertising through circulars such as this one. (Circular, Thomas Ormsby, Commission Bureau and General Purchasing Agency, 1861; courtesy American Antiquarian Society) every part of Woman's Form, and showing her Perfect Capacities for the Purposes of Love, Procreative Duties and Happiness." Ormsby guaranteed readers "wishing many articles that can only be procured in New York City" that he could ship anywhere. With New York closely linked in readers' minds to the trade in erotica, "articles that can only be procured in New York City" served as code for readers looking for explicit images and books—here the city served the same purpose as noms du plume such as Paul de Kock or Butt Ender, the author of many New York City brothel guides. Ormsby did not list the racier titles with which he had been associated previously, but assuring readers of "his long experience" with such matters, he guaranteed that they would not be disappointed with his selections.[25]

Another circular offered an impressive list of illustrated "Genuine Fancy Books" ranging in price from $1 to $3, many of which had been named in previous indictments of men who were selling "lewd, wicked, scandalous, infamous, and obscene printed books"—the ubiquitous *Fanny Hill*, for instance, but also *Silas Shovewell and His Amours with Nuns*, and *Curtains Drawn Up, or the Education of Laura*. According to the circular, each book featured five to ten colored illustrations, and none were available for sale at the proprietor's New York office. "All orders must be sent by mail," the dealer instructed, and orders would "be sent either by *Mail or Express*, with perfect safety, and done up in such a matter to defy detection."[26] The circular is not associated with any particular shop, but the layout allowed the vendor to pencil in price reductions from the shop's established prices in order to encourage sales.[27]

Despite assurances, sending books and racy papers through the mail did not always guarantee their secure arrival. Ackerman complained on several occasions of postal workers "confiscating" *Venus Miscellany* for their own personal use. "Now if these postmasters *who rifle the mails*, will allow us their names, we will send them our paper gratis," Ackerman promised *Miscellany* readers in January 1857, "provided they will let those belonging to subscribers alone."[28] Police exposed the workings of this new mail order trade when in September they staked out the post office near Ackerman's office on Nassau Street. "He visited the Post Office three times each day," the *New York Herald* reported, "and regularly received over fifty letters at a time, which contained orders for his vile sheet and other indecent publications, accompanied by postage stamps and bills to the amount demanded for them."[29] Upon investigation, police found out that postal clerks were well aware of the nature of Ackerman's business— perhaps they too were offered free copies. Ackerman was arrested, but he was released, again, on assurances to the district attorney that he would stop publishing the paper.[30] Although erotica dealers operated on the margins of the law, they exhibited little concern for their prosecution outside of New York City—for successful and well-connected entrepreneurs like Ackerman, there was little reason even to fear it locally.

Focused on providing materials through the mail, New York's erotica dealers made use of the opportunities provided by the war. The porn business benefited from technological innovations such as the carte de visite—photographs affixed to card stock that measured around two by four inches, were intended for exchanging, and that were easily stored in a pocket—and stereograph, but improvements to mail delivery offered entrepreneurs the national audience they most wanted. Congress maintained low postal rates for mail sent to the U.S. Army, special franking privileges allowed much needed supplies to reach the troops, and by 1862 mail was sorted and moved on specially designed railroad cars (fig. 4).[31] Letters and supplies sent from home moved quickly and cheaply during the war, reaching men in camp and on the move. Men wrote letters home asking for food, items of clothing, and mementos; New York's erotica dealers hoped that they would also place orders for racy books and images. Alongside letters from home and supplies intended for the troops, booksellers' circulars advertised the latest in published erotica, safely and conveniently packaged and sent directly to the front. Erotica dealers were not alone in recognizing the great opportunity in the concentration of men in army camps and their easy accessibility. The U.S.

Fig. 4. Erotica dealers took advantage of fast and cheap mail delivery offered by train during the war. ("Interior of Railroad Car," *Frank Leslie's Magazine*, October 6, 1888, 124)

Christian Commission created a portable loan library, a collection of right reading materials sent out to hundreds of hospitals and camps — books that might once have shared space in the very same mail bags that carried "yellow-covered literature."[32]

If army correspondence is any indication, the strategy worked. There seems to have been no shortage of obscene materials available and widely circulated among and to soldiers during the Civil War. An anonymous soldier addressed himself to a Philadelphia newspaper in August 1861 complaining of men "reading flimsy publications, obscene books, and the worst species of yellow-covered literature," turning their minds into "dingy cloisters, filled with cobwebs and the death-damps of grovelling desires."[33] In the early months of the war men could have acquired the erotica at any number of depots, tucking it into boots, hats, or jacket pockets. Later on, and farther afield, however, obscene pictures and books seemed to become even more plentiful, suggesting that items of erotica reached the men through the mail. Writing from Northern Virginia in June 8, 1863, general and provost marshal Marsena Rudolph Patrick recorded in his diary that he "seized upon and now hold[s], large amounts of Bogus Jewelry, Watches, etc. all from the same houses that furnish the vilest of Obscene Books, of which I have made a great haul lately."[34] The *Philadelphia Inquirer* approved of Patrick's cleanup efforts in Washington, complaining that "the mail privileges to the Army of the Potomac have been greatly abused" by parties sending "lots of obscene books, gift packages and other articles of similar character."[35] Not all erotica was circulated through the mail. An August 1862 letter addressed to a New York newspaper from Fredericksburg, Virginia, described "Army Leeches" and "Fancy Men," who while young and "able to bear arms" instead descend on camp in "squads of six, twelve, & c... with obscene books and prints, and soon fill the camps with their dangerous trash."[36]

The problem was not reserved to the eastern theater, for the following spring Captain M. G. Tousley addressed a complaint from Blue Springs, Tennessee, describing his frustrated efforts. "Obscene prints and photographs," Tousley explained, "such as are quite commonly kept and exhibited by soldiers and even officers, add greatly to the unavoidable influences that thus demoralize." Even more than the books and pictures were the circulars, which Tousley explained "are continuously distributed in large numbers to 1st and 2nd Lieut[enants] and Orderlies of all companies in the service." Distributed freely among the men, circulars with suggestive titles, Tousley worried, could demoralize the men. As when the district attorney in New York read titles into the record, Tousley's complaint about the danger of "improper" catalogs or circulars relied on listeners' erotic imaginations or a shared knowledge of what constituted the obscene. Titles like noms de plumes served as code, and readers familiar with one story might be able to fill in the details of another from the title.

Under these circumstances, soldiers would have been hard pressed to *avoid* porn, much less refrain from acquiring it. Tousley intended to send the offending circulars to officials in New York, but fearing their "negligence or complicity," he addressed his letter to the president and included an "Improper Circular" just in case.[37] Tousley apparently saw no irony in sending the obscene circular through the U.S. Mail, even though it would once again pass through the hands of an orderly, a sutler or two, and mail carriers, who had helped to deliver it in the first place.

Colonel Lafayette Baker, serving with the wartime secret service charged with policing vice in the capital, recalled when "his attention was attracted to a fruitful source of gain at the expense of virtue, and even decency: the traffic in corrupt literature and art." The man charged with breaking up notorious district brothels—and who would later help apprehend the Lincoln assassination conspirators—nonetheless claimed that he knew "of no lower grade of depravity than that of this shameless business. The vile book, photograph, and wood-cut, were scattered by sutlers, mail agents, and others, throughout the army." Predicting the cautionary tales that Comstock related about the "Young Person" fallen victim to porn, Baker suspected that these materials ruined "the morals and bodies of men" of the U.S. Army. The publishers of these works, men whom Baker called "human vampires," prayed on men far from home, using as their weapon of choice the U.S. Mail—the very same medium used by mothers, fathers, and wives to entreat men to be good. Receiving assurances from Postmaster General Montgomery Blair that the matter was under consideration, Baker began a massive confiscation of obscene materials in and around Washington. Baker collected an estimated twenty-two thousand dollars' worth of goods, made "a bonfire of this pile of sensual trash" outside of the White House, and invited President Lincoln to watch. Whether "our pure minded President" did indeed come and "enjoy the sight," as Baker recalled, we cannot know, but in the aftermath of Lincoln's assassination, Baker liked to remember the president lending his imprimatur to the project.³⁸

Anecdotal reports such as these suggest that the particular circumstances of the U.S. Civil War made possible the triumph of pornography, with its influence reaching into the ranks of enlisted men and officers, collapsing the distance between men who owned porn and those who sold or distributed it. Obscene images and books reached Congress, were directed to the President's desk, and were stacked and set aflame on the White House lawn. Threading through these early concerns for the easy accessibility of erotic publications is a tension between the implied assumption that those concerned shared an understanding of what constituted the obscene and the need to define it, name it, or exhibit it. Why read the titles of the books into the official record or keep a copy of an obscene circular to send to President Lincoln? Because by midcentury that consensus was breaking down, first stretched thin by the antebellum trade in erotica and now buckling under the pressure of a war-born explosion of porn. Lynn Hunt has suggested that pornography was *invented* in the nineteenth century, in courtrooms and other places where people sought to regulate it. Reformers and officials, Hunt explains, invented the category in response to a democratization of culture.³⁹ "Pornography names an argument," Walter Kendrick has explained, "not a thing." As such, pornography would never name the erotica held in "gentlemen's collections" but applied instead to an argument against books, pictures, and other items intended for wide consumption.⁴⁰

Pornography would also never name works written and published by the period's antislavery luminaries, Theodore Dwight Weld, for instance, or Harriet Beecher Stowe, yet antislavery authors were concerned that readers might not draw sharp enough distinctions. Historian Karen Halttunen has argued that reform literature reflected changes in popular erotica, which by the early nineteenth century portrayed sexual fantasies that included pain—flagellation, for instance. Intended to enlist readers to abolition, antislavery authors portrayed scenes of the flogging of slaves that eroticized pain, "constructing it as sexual in nature."[41] In Weld's *American Slavery as It Is: Testimony of a Thousand Witnesses,* a witness recalled slave mistresses beating their slaves, describing how "their sensibility changed to fury must needs feed itself for a while on the hideous spectacle; they must, as if to revive themselves, hear the piercing shrieks, and see the flow of fresh blood; there are some of them who, in their frantic rage, pinch and bite their victims."[42] The South was regularly compared to a brothel or harem, furthering this association between sex and violence.[43]

Antislavery authors fended off criticisms that they were appealing to readers' base instincts by employing strategic omission—a tool used to great effect in period erotica—and by coaching readers to be disgusted by what they read. Stowe's *Uncle Tom's Cabin* used both strategies. "Scenes of blood and cruelty are shocking to our ear and heart," Stowe explained in the scene in which Tom is being beaten to death.[44] In repeated references, Stowe appealed to "the reader," instructing them in how to respond to the cruelty and violence unfolding before their eyes. "While this scene was going on in the men's sleeping-room," Stowe wrote about a slave auction, "the reader might be interested to take a peep at the corresponding apartment allotted to women"; readers who "peeped" were treated to an emotionally intimate scene between the beautiful fifteen-year-old slave, Emmeline, and her mother, about to be sold, followed by the auction intended to shock and sicken readers.[45] Antislavery authors and their defenders were painfully aware, though, that readers made their own sense of these scenes. "You will confer a favor on the public," an interested reader wrote to a Washington, D.C., paper, "by hinting to the publishers of Mrs. Stowe's great work that a cheap edition of 'Uncle Tom's Cabin' would be acceptably received."[46] Surely the publishers could release a copy made on cheaper paper and offer it for well under a dollar.

Authors of period erotica employed the same tactics in offering readers brief glimpses and disclaiming any ill intentions. "We shall not offend the reader's good taste by describing the disgusting caresses that followed," George Thompson, a.k.a. Greenhorn, a.k.a. Charles Paul de Kock, intimated in *City Crimes*, in the midst of a dungeon sex scene between Julia, a young beautiful white woman, and a slave named Nero; "suffice it to say, that the interview was commenced in a manner as might have been expected under the circumstances." Thompson found in contemporary accounts of slavery inspiration for his erotica; Julia, for instance, goes on to fantasize about finding a rich man whom she can make "my slave."[47] Authors of antebellum erotica imagined the erotic possibilities of interracial sex, or "amalgamation," as contemporaries would refer to it. Scenes that included interracial sex accompanied by violence, explicit or implicit, suggest that antislavery writing both absorbed and contributed to an expansion of the antebellum erotic imagination.

Searching for a word to condemn publishers of erotica, Colonel Baker's imagination settled on "human vampires," a term used by slavery's opponents to describe slavery and slave owners. Abolitionists compared slave owners to vampires or referred to the institution of slavery as "the vampire." "If we had any regard for our safety and happiness," William Lloyd Garrison entreated listeners at an American Colonization Society meeting, "we should strive to crush the Vampire which is feeding upon our life-blood."[48] An article in the *Liberator* condemned Daniel Webster's support for the 1850 Fugitive Slave Law in the following terms: "The spirit of freedom having left Webster, every drop of the blood of humanity being drawn from his veins, the vampire of slavery took possession of the corpse."[49] And, of course, in the midst of beating their slaves, Weld's frenzied female slaveholders bit them. Slave owners were compared to bloodhounds and reptiles even, but for critics of slavery vampires seemed to capture its complete lack of restraint. So too did it work to describe those who would pray on U.S. soldiers, selling them images and yellow-covered tracts that drained them of their ability to fight and ill-fitted them for life at home.

Fig. 5. Abolitionists helped shape an antebellum erotic imagination when they invoked scenes of illicit sex. Critics employed similar conventions when they condemned abolitionists for encouraging race mixing. Artist Edward W. Clay created a series of prints titled *Practical Amalgamation*, including this one, in response to Theodore Dwight Weld and Angelina Grimké's 1838 marriage ceremony attended by both black and white guests. (Edward Clay, "Amalgamation Waltz," New York, John Childs, 1839; courtesy American Antiquarian Society)

Antislavery tracts and erotica were produced for two distinct audiences, but conventions employed and subjects covered by both formed part of an antebellum erotic imagination that confounded efforts to build a consensus on what constituted the obscene. Seeking words to condemn one meant borrowing from the other, and in the push and pull middle-class reformers added to a lexicon of sexually explicit talk. Antislavery authors were regularly condemned and violently attacked for being racial and sexual iconoclasts, perhaps none more so than Weld, "the most mobbed man in America." When Weld and Angelina Grimké invited black guests to their wedding in Philadelphia in 1838, the event was lampooned in newspapers, broadsheets, and prints; for example, "An Amalgamation Waltz," one of a series of prints titled *Practical Amalgamation*, portrayed leering men dining and dancing with women of the opposite race, their bodies arranged in a number of suggestive positions (fig. 5).[50] And, when this did not make the point, a "mob" burned down the antislavery meeting hall where Grimké and others spoke.

Buried under a mountain of obscene publications, lawmakers and U.S. Army whistle-blowers sought to build a consensus about what constituted pornography. Key to the argument was establishing that items marked as porn were named, exhibited, and circulated with the intention to corrupt the minds—and perhaps destroy the bodies—of youth. John Atchison, you may recall, was indicted for "intending the morals of the Youth . . . to corrupt." Captain Tousley complained about obscene circulars that had the tendency to "demoralize" the troops, and to Lafayette Baker erotica dealers were "human vampires" who preyed on the "morals and bodies of men." The "great evil" identified by senators debating the 1865 prohibition was that these items were "sent here and there and everywhere," an influence from which youth had to be protected. "Our youth are in danger," Comstock declared in the preface to his 1883 *Traps for the Young*, but by then the point hardly needed saying. But who were these "youth" who needed protecting? This "Young Person," Kendrick suggests, "lived only in the nervous imagination of men inhabiting a particular class and historical moment."[51] Union soldiers were in their early twenties, on average, slightly younger than their Confederate counterparts and significantly less likely to have children of their own.[52] Those who sent them off to fight imagined the men of the U.S. Army more as sons than husbands. Begun in local prosecution and coming of age in the Civil War, American pornography came to be associated with the experience of soldiering. The endangered "youth" at times served as shorthand for the fighting men and for class prerogatives that pornography threatened to upset.

When the Civil War began, the domestic trade in pornography was well established, and entrepreneurial publishers/dealers were posed to take advantage of the war's particular circumstances and new technologies and mediums. Nurtured in the transatlantic context, American antipornography had realized some success by quietly seeking federal support. In the meantime, yellow-covered literature, obscene circulars, and racy magazines made their way with or to the soldiers and became part of the sexual culture of U.S. Army camps.

TWO

STORMING THE ENEMY'S BREASTWORKS

Civil War Courts-Martial and the Sexual Culture of the U.S. Army Camp

Colonel Ebenezer Peirce had commanded the Twenty-Ninth Regiment, Massachusetts Volunteers, for about seven weeks when in April 1862 he found himself in the middle of court-martial proceedings, defending himself from a number of charges, including "conduct unbecoming an officer and a gentleman." The violations under this specification that Peirce was charged with included striking a private without cause, disguising himself and sneaking out of camp to keep company with a disreputable woman, and reading aloud to privates in his company from a popular erotic book.[1] *Fanny Hill, or Memoirs of a Woman of Pleasure*, by John Cleland, originally published in England in 1748 (and never out of print since), features the story of a naïve country girl lured into a life of prostitution in London. *Fanny Hill*—which was mistakenly referred to as *"Francis Hill"* during the trial or more often simply by the more descriptive secondary title, *Memoirs of a Woman of Pleasure*—was virtually required stock for antebellum dealers in erotica. The book was named in the Atchison, Ormsby, and Ackerman indictments mentioned in chapter 1.

Fanny Hill consists of a series of letters written by the protagonist to another woman in which Fanny describes the wide range of sexual activities she engages in as a prostitute, including "sex between women, cross-dressing, flagellation, orgies, and public sex."[2] By midcentury, cheap domestically produced copies of *Fanny Hill* featuring crude engravings were available for less than a dollar, while more lavishly illustrated versions of the classic, like the one described in the circular dating to the 1860s pictured in chapter 1 (see fig. 2), featuring twenty-four "colored plates," sold for a few dollars (fig. 6). We cannot know which version was circulated among the men of the Twenty-Ninth Regiment, Massachusetts Volunteers, because the book was never admitted into evidence, though the men involved discussed its contents often during the eleven-day trial. Indeed, although the book served as damning evidence against Peirce, no one ever discussed the book's current whereabouts, nor did U.S. Army officers evince any interest in confiscating it. Like the witnesses called to the prosecution, Peirce's copy of *Fanny Hill*—or Private William McFarland's, Private Daniel Blaisdell's, or whoever it belonged to—was chiefly of interest for what it had to say about the accused. Assuming the book in question remained at large, the men of the Twenty-Ninth had continued to circulate it and enjoy reading about the sexual exploits of an eighteenth-century English prostitute.[3]

Peirce surely never anticipated sitting in a courtroom in which his fellow army officers weighed in on his choice of reading material, much less having to defend himself from accusations of conduct unbecoming an officer. Born into a Massachusetts family of some wealth and a graduate of New England's finest private academies, Peirce followed others of his class into the army.[4] He was appointed colonel of the Twenty-Ninth in December 1861, a move that angered others in the regiment who had anticipated one of their own being elevated to that post. Throughout the proceedings, Peirce insisted that he was a victim of "an unrighteous effort" to "disgrace my character and compel my resignation," including having false accusations leveled against him by those who resented his appointment as colonel, and that the charges of misconduct were grossly unfair.[5] The book *Fanny Hill* was indeed in his tent, but it belonged to one of his orderlies, Peirce insisted. And, he "manifested a becoming indignation at finding it in his quarters."[6]

But the testimony of others in his regiment tells a different story, of men sharing the vices of the army camp and of an outsider offi-

Fig. 6. By the mid-nineteenth century, *Fanny Hill* was available in a wide variety of forms, including versions with lavish illustrations such as these two. Illustrations brought to life various scenes in the book about the sexual exploits of a naïve country girl lured into a life of prostitution in London, including sex between women and sex in public. (*Fanny Hill, or Memoirs of a Woman of Pleasure*, 1830, n.p.; courtesy Kinsey Institute)

cer trying to substitute likability for respect. Not only did his men describe incidents when their colonel sneaked past the picket line in disguise and read aloud from period pornography, but on at least one occasion, they alleged, Peirce called privates to his tent where he encouraged them to sing bawdy songs with suggestive lyrics for his own enjoyment and that of his fellow officers. Peirce characterized this charge as "unwarranted and unmanly" and insisted that the songs were not vulgar but "harmless."[7] Military authorities intent on ascertaining the titles and content of the songs pushed witnesses to remember particular lyrics so that they might themselves recall the titles. The judge advocate general pressed Lieutenant Thomas A. Mayo on this point when Mayo recalled that one song was about "a gentleman putting his hand where the curly hair grows." "Was it curly hair or curly locks?" Mayo was asked, to which he responded, "Curly locks, I think." "Was the song called the Farmer's daughter?," and Mayo answered, "I think that was one of them."[8]

In the exchange about lyrics and titles, the judge advocate general and the lieutenant drew from common cultural reference points. That the suggestive songs and erotica shared among the Massachusetts men encamped at Newport News, Virginia, were familiar to the officers involved in the court-martial proceedings — colonels hailing from various Indiana, New York, and Maryland regiments — worked decidedly against Peirce's denials and claims of ignorance and innocence. Military men bonded with one another as they shared in the various vices that ran through the camps, so when a soldier enlisted in a Massachusetts regiment could not recall the title of a bawdy song, another one connected to an Indiana regiment could help him out. Vices such as liquor, prostitutes, and pornography served as social levelers, uniting men in their shared transgressions of the domestic ideal. The voyeurism and objectification of Civil War pornography helped to create what Lynn Hunt has described, in a different context, as a "new fraternity" among the officers and men in the ranks of the U.S. Army.[9] Exchanging and sharing erotic words and images formed part of the sexual culture of the camps in which officers and enlisted men implicitly agreed to ways of seeing women and one another implied in period pornography. The ideals of pornography were strongly opposed to domesticity, which relied on female sexual difference and male restraint. So, too, did soldiering, which required violence and a denial of difference. Pornography, it could be said, helped make good soldiers, allowing men to build fraternal bonds across rank and region. But when a man fell short as a soldier, his involvement in pornography proved useful to those who sought to discipline him. Using the records of the U.S. Army Courts-Martial, in this chapter I describe how men acquired and circulated obscene images and literature, and by placing this material in the sexual culture of the camps, I consider what meaning they might have made of it.[10]

Existing summaries of some of the titles offered on the *Genuine Fancy Books* catalog alongside *Fanny Hill* (see fig. 2) give us some sense of the items available to men serving in the Union Army, and if there is truth to guilt by association, perhaps of some of the items circulating among the men. The title *Rose de Amor*, featured a Frenchman who creates an Ottoman-style harem in the French countryside, and although no description is available for *Lustful Turk*, it likely covered the same sexual terrain.[11] Among men living in a world without women, it is not difficult to imagine the attraction of reading about men surrounded by willing women. The opposite scenario is implied in the title *Silas Shovewell, His Amours with the Nuns*. Although no summary of this work could be found, the title identifies it within the genre of nativist exposés such as the *Awful Disclosures of Maria Monk* detailing the sexual exploits of priests and nuns. The two other titles for which some information on content could be found are *Curtain Drawn Up, or The Education of Laura* and the *Cicily Martin, the Woman of Pleasure*. Both titles feature female protagonists narrating a process of sexual self-discovery. *The Education of Laura* derived from a French story of a young woman eagerly watching a variety of sexual acts in which the narrator makes thinly veiled references to female masturbation, such as when she admits to "procuring

[for] myself each day the most delicious sensations of pleasure."[12] Elizabeth Hawley dates the original publication of *Cicily Martin* to 1846. *Cicily Martin* follows the same narrative as *Fanny Hill*, except here the young naïve country girl is lured to New York with the promise of respectable work and finds herself working in a brothel instead. Like *Fanny Hill*, the rest of the novel is about the girl's sexual exploits with her elite clientele (fig. 7), including several who enjoy flagellation.[13] Like other works produced in the antebellum period, in the end Cicily chooses a life of virtue over that of vice, a common trope for antebellum novels such as these.

The latter two titles share with *Fanny Hill* a strong strain of voyeurism, of listening in on a young woman's private revelations to a female confessor. Although both celebrated women's sexuality, the stories offered up women's bodies as a means of male bonding. In his court-martial trial, much was made of the charge that Ebenezer Peirce read aloud from Fanny Hill's confessions to soldiers beneath him in rank, but no one was surprised when the men in the courtroom expressed a shared familiarity with the sexual life of a British prostitute. Written in the first person, the books seem ideal for reading aloud, and Peirce's trial records suggested that these works were shared widely among the men.

When Private William McFarland, Peirce's former orderly, testified that he saw "Colonel Peirce at two different times once in the day time and once at night reading a book with bawdy pictures in it," the judge advocate general asked him how he knew the title of the book. McFarland responded that he saw it and that a lieutenant came in to borrow it while Peirce was out and then found it on Colonel Peirce's desk.[14] Peirce's own witnesses claimed to have seen the book in various hands of officers and enlisted men and on the ledge of a tent, under another private's mattress, and alternately on top of Peirce's desk and in a drawer, either open or closed.[15] Little wonder one of the charges leveled against Peirce was that he failed to competently drill his men, for they seem to have been preoccupied with exploring the sexual exploits of a female prostitute. All of this leaves the impres-

Fig. 7. *Cicily Martin* followed a story line similar to that of *Fanny Hill*, except that the former naïve country girl experiences her sexual awakening in New York, where she winds up working at a brothel. (*The Life and Adventures of Cicily Martin*, 1846, after p. 184; courtesy American Antiquarian Society)

sion that the book was shared and borrowed—or, alternately, that *Fanny Hill* was standard issue among the men of the Twenty-Ninth Massachusetts—and that it made little sense to connect it exclusively to Peirce.

The copy of *Fanny Hill* making its rounds among the men of the Twenty-Ninth Massachusetts at camp in the Virginia Peninsula appears to have been generously illustrated, making it accessible to men who did not read or those who preferred to substitute their own fantasy narratives for Fanny Hill's confessions. Three different witnesses described the images in the book, some in more detail than others. On the tenth day of the trial, the court asked James Boothe, Colonel Peirce's current orderly, to describe the book in question. "It was a vulgar book," Boothe replied, but when asked if he had ever read it, Boothe said no. So the court pressed the issue, asking, "How do you know it is a vulgar book if you never read it?," to which Boothe responded, "I saw the first picture in it." Digging for more specifics, the court asked what kind, to which Boothe replied, "It was a woman with her legs open. She was all bare." Hoping to cast doubt on Boothe, who had been called to testify in defense of Peirce, the court asked, "Can you read?," to which the orderly answered, "Yes sir."[16] Although this last question was related to an earlier part of Boothe's testimony regarding his claim to seeing orders dismissing Private McFarland for bringing the book to Peirce's quarters, it underscored the point that erotica circulating in U.S. Army camps could be enjoyed on multiple levels—clearly one did not have to be literate to enjoy a book such as this. But the court, eager to discipline Peirce, would have found it easier to dismiss Boothe's defense of the colonel had the orderly been unable to read the title of the book in question.

Also, soldiers did not have to read to sample the wide range of erotic images available to them, some of them produced for the specific circumstances of the war. Whereas *Fanny Hill*, *Cicily Martin*, and the range of other fancy books advertised in period circulars were often recycled or revised from European originals, new printing and imaging technologies made it possible for manufacturers to produce items designed specifically to appeal to men fighting in the war.[17] The circular Captain M. G. Tousley enclosed in his March 1864 letter to Lincoln, mentioned in chapter 1, describes a number of suggestive images available to the men of Company E, Eighty-Fourth Regiment, Illinois Infantry, in camp at Blue Springs, Tennessee. Titled "New Pictures for Bachelors," the dealer's circular promised twelve- by fifteen-inch images, "highly colored and fit for framing, for twelve cents a piece, or a dozen for $1.20." Buyers interested in the discount could buy twelve of the same image, presumably for sharing, or they could chose an assortment selected from "Behind the Scenes," "A Bed-room Bombardment," "The Wood Nymphs' Frolic," "The Temptation of St. Anthony," "Circessian Slaves," "The Maiden's Retreat," "Jack and the Mermaids," "Toilet Mysteries," "Girls Bathing," and one titled "Storming the Enemy's Breastworks." The condition of women in Turkish harems, or "circessian slaves," proved to be endlessly interesting to antebellum Americans, and the newspapers covered the topic in lavish detail, as they did with antislavery literature, in articles that mingled fascination with disgust. One such article on a well-attended lecture, provocatively titled "A Night in a Harem," titillated readers with a description of the husband lifting his wife's veil on their wedding night: "The preliminaries arranged, he enters the chamber of the bride and finds her on the sofa, veiled."[18] Nonwhite women as subjects of sexual conquest were featured in such books as *Lustful Turk* and *Rose de Amor* described above. Descriptions of images advertised to soldiers in camp need not have gone much further than the newspapers to tap the antebellum erotic imagination and conjure the exotic picture of young veiled enslaved women reclining on sofas.

The last title on the list, "Storming the Enemy's Breastworks," might have had special appeal to men in the third year of the war. The short description of the print promised that the picture featured "an amorous Union soldier . . . playing with a Secesh maiden, making a very indelicate assault," which the unsuspecting girl tries half-heartedly to ward off. "Under the circumstances," the description teases, "we must conclude that the Breastworks unconditionally surrendered."[19] With its focus on military and sexual conquest, this image was unique in a list that featured pastoral pictures of women bathing, dressing, and sleepwalking, all far removed in time and place from the war the men were fighting. Whereas the other titles took men's erotic imaginations far from the battlefield, "Storming" turned the battlefield into erotic terrain, populated not by willing concubines or the unknowing schoolgirls of "A Bed-room Bombardment" but by feminized Confederates who while not altogether unwilling prove incapable of resisting. "Storming the Enemy's Breastworks" reflected months of popular anger expressed in the North and echoed civilian calls to escalate the war as it entered its fourth year; by then, papers were calling not just for victory but for retribution. In spring 1864, when Tousley forwarded the circular to Lincoln, northern papers reported widespread neglect and abuse of U.S. prisoners in Confederate prisons, and that summer *Frank Leslie's* and *Harper's Weekly* published shocking pictures of naked and emaciated prisoners of war that were greeted with loud calls for revenge against southern civilians. Unmediated even by an invented female voice, the pictures advertised in the "Bachelors" circular—of women either unwilling or unknowing—reflect the all-male milieu in which they were made and were intended to be consumed. But they also communicated anger felt at home and a willingness to represent retributive sexual violence as desirable. The widely circulated postmortem lithographs of Helen Jewett—a prostitute whose 1836 murder was covered in lurid detail in New York's sporting press—had proved that there was profit to be had in eroticized violence and, as was the case in the murder trial that ensued, no repercussions for the perpetrators (fig. 8).[20]

Second Lieutenant William Lyman of the Thirteenth New York Heavy Artillery faced a long list of charges under Specification 2, conduct unbecoming an officer and a gentleman; having and sharing obscene books and cartes de visite were not the most serious. Nonetheless, members of his court-martial found the testimony compelling

Courts-Martial and the Sexual Culture of the U.S. Army Camp 43

Fig. 8. New York printer Henry R. Robinson created a series of lithographs in response to the 1836 murder of Helen Jewett. Like this one, the illustrations emphasized Jewett's sexual allure, even in death. ("Ellen Jewett, 1836"; courtesy American Antiquarian Society)

enough to find him guilty on all counts, including possessing pornography, and to recommend dismissal. At camp in Fort Hamilton in New York Harbor, Lyman was in the habit of inviting women into his tent for sex, and his fellow officers were in the habit of peeking into his tent and catching him in the act. One witness at his court-martial testified that he and several other officers were visiting the lieutenant in his tent one evening in March 1864 when a book lying on Lyman's table caught the attention of one of them. "I have something that will beat that," the witness recalled Lyman saying; then he took out and "showed us some cartes de visite of ladies in every shape, undressed, some of them had men and women both in them, obscene pictures" (fig. 9). The lieutenant, acting as his own council, asked the witness for the title of the book in question, perhaps as a way to take the court's attention away from the obscene cartes de visite. The witness

Fig. 9. Cartes de visite featuring close-ups of women's bodies, such as the ones shown here, were widely available and were named in the court-martial proceedings against Second Lieutenant William Lyman, Thirteenth New York Heavy Artillery. Cartes such as these formed part of a sexual culture that placed a premium on visual access. (Lowry, *Story the Soldiers Wouldn't Tell*, after p. 83; reprinted with permission)

recalled no details about the book, explaining that—even with everything else going on around him—he was reading a newspaper.[21] Unlike in Peirce's trial, some of Lyman's fellow officers seemed intent on keeping the cartes away from the enlisted men, for a private testified to an awkward conversation in which another officer accused *him* of having seen Lyman's cartes, to which the soldier indignantly replied that he had seen cartes of "an improper nature . . . many times."[22] Lyman, apparently, was not the only source of cartes de visite featuring naked women, but in the midst of the court-martial proceedings Lyman's pornography became part of the damning evidence marshaled against him.

Two such cartes des visite are included in Thomas Lowry's collection *The Story the Soldiers Wouldn't Tell*: one of a naked woman's back and another of a woman's front (fig. 9). Lowry dates both to the period, although he does not—indeed, we cannot—place them in anyone's hands. Not surprisingly, the cartes are not credited to a particular photographer; both are held privately by collectors who have vouched for their midcentury origins. Reproducing the through-the-peephole access that men in the camps demanded of one another, midcentury obscene cartes de visite featured close-ups of female genitalia. Although artists had long been fascinated with female sexuality, it was photography, art historian Kelly Dennis explains, that invented the beaver shot.[23] Collapsing the distance between seeing and touching, cartes were mass produced, small enough to be tucked into a book or stored in a pocket, affixed to firm backing, and, unlike framed photographs, intended to be handled. Henry Ward Beecher warned young men about "EVIL BOOKS" and "EVIL PICTURES," which he lumped together as "black-lettered literature" that "is fingered and read nightly, and hatches in the young mind broods of salacious thoughts."[24] Handling suggestive images was an intensely tactile experience, according to Beecher, one that elicited a powerful bodily effect.

Historians have remarked on the "cartomania" that gripped the country during the war. Encouraged by the low price of producing

Fig. 10. An unknown Union soldier sat for this photo and may have planned this prank in advance. (Carte de visite, in the possession of Thomas Lowry; reprinted with permission)

multiple copies of an image at one time and expanded access to professional photographers, Americans of all sorts sat for pictures and collected the mass-produced cartes de visite of famous celebrities. The two images from Lowry's collection were likely taken of performers or prostitutes and sold en masse by the photographer or a vendor. Historian J. Matthew Gallman points out that soldiers regularly sat for pictures and shared them with friends and family—they were $2 or $3 a dozen, or less than one week's pay for a Union soldier.[25] The Union soldier who sat for the carte de visite in figure 10 likely enlisted the cooperation of the photographer in what appears to have been a prank, a formal pose with an open fly. But who would have been the likely recipients of these cartes? Wives and sweethearts regularly wrote requesting photographs of absentee men to keep by their bedsides or to share with their children. "I would like very much if you had got some photographs taken and sent me some and an album to put them in," Sarah Neel, a young pregnant mother of four young children living north of Pittsburgh, wrote to her husband.[26] "I hope that you look as well as your likeness," Alice Waddell of Wilkes Barre, Pennsylvania, wrote to her husband, William, "for

Fig. 11. Civil War soldiers went together to be photographed and sometimes posed together. (Reproduction no. LC-USZ62-65089 [b&w film copy neg.]; Prints and Photographs Division, Library of Congress)

[I] think that you look much better then when you left home."[27] Although couples shared intimate fantasies in letters sent to and from home, with homes full of toddlers, Neel or Waddell might have found a carte such as figure 10 more appropriate for a pocket than a mantel.

The pose in figure 10 reflects the male milieu in which it was created. Few photographers were female, and soldiers often went together to have their photos taken, sometimes even posing together for their photographs. The photography studio or the makeshift camp setting, then, reproduced the camp milieu; photographs like those in figures 11 and 12 served as a testament to comradery and trust. The photo of two unidentified Union soldiers posing in front of a painted backdrop, with weapons drawn, was perhaps planned ahead of time or at least choreographed once the men found themselves in front of the camera (fig. 13). It is not clear if any planning or choreogra-

Fig. 12. Soldiers un-self-consciously posed with arms draped over each other's shoulders, reflecting an uncomplicated emotional intimacy. (LC-DIG-ppmsca-27254 [digital file from original item]; Prints and Photographs Division, Library of Congress)

phy preceded the unnamed soldier in the photograph from Thomas Lowry's collection (fig. 10) or if the soldier acted spontaneously in making a carte de visite that revealed something of the culture in which it was produced. In the camps, men looked and were watched. Thomas Wentworth Higginson once compared interactions of men in the army to "the felicity of Adam and Eve," recalling an occasion when he emerged from a swim with "not even a rag to which a button by any earthly possibility could be appended" and encountered a sentry who "dutifully saluted his naked colonel."[28] Expressions of emotional intimacy were a common feature of Victorian correspondence, and the feelings behind these expressions are captured in wartime photographs in which men pose un-self-consciously together, arms

Fig. 13. Soldiers posing for a choreographed photograph. (Reproduction no. LC-DIG-ppmsca-37138 [digital file from original, tonality adjusted], LC-DIG-ppmsca-27138 [digital file from original item]; Prints and Photographs Division, Library of Congress)

absently draped around each other (fig. 12). In his study of World War I, historian Paul Fussell described the love men felt for one another in the trenches as "front-line homoeroticism."[29] Among antebellum Americans, feelings of affection expressed in words, images, or touches reaffirmed period notions of manliness and fraternal love and, within the context of war's violence, worked "in opposition to and as a triumph over death."[30]

Whatever the content of Lieutenant Lyman's cartes des visite, it is notable that, unlike the materials held by Colonel Peirce or the men in Captain Tousley's command, these obscene cartes de visite were circulated among men who were not encamped far from home. Lyman was from New York City and, indeed, claimed that one of the

Fig. 14. Soldiers displayed images of women taken from illustrated newspapers in their quarters as a means of comfort. (Fashion plates, *Godey's Lady's Book*, April 1861, after p. 180, and April 1864, before p. 325; courtesy Van Pelt Library, University of Pennsylvania)

women found in his bed was a "virtuous" friend from home. That is not to say, of course, that the men were not homesick but rather that, unsurprisingly, pornography was part of life in camp. Lyman, at least, seems to have *tried* to have sex with real women and, along with his fellow officers, fantasized about them, too. New research on rape in the war reminds us that Union soldiers away from home fulfilled desires by seeking nonconsensual sex. Historians Susan Barber and Charles Ritter, for instance, studied more than 450 courts-martial for rape in the occupied territory, a number that likely only scratches the surface of such assaults. Barber and Ritter show that the U.S. Army took rape accusations seriously and gave victims the space to seek justice. The authors argue that rape, though representing a small percentage of crimes heard in military courts, was "among the most frequently prosecuted civilian crimes tried by the military."[31]

Homesickness inspired Lieutenant Thomas Galwey to look for and share pictures of women. Encamped in Falmouth, Virginia, during the winter of 1862–63 after tough fights at Antietam and Fredericksburg, Galwey and others in the Eighth Ohio Volunteer Infantry covered the walls of their crude huts with pictures cut from illustrated newspapers. "What are most sought after," Galwey explained in his journal, "are the colored fashion plates in the ladies' magazines."[32] Although not the only ladies' magazine of the period, the popular monthly *Godey's Lady's Book* featured a hand-tinted fashion plate on its cover, which might have been what Galwey and his men were referencing (fig. 14). The next winter he clipped images from *Leslie's Lady's Magazine* and bought various other illustrated magazines from the sutler, affixing these to the walls of his hut. "The colored fashion plates will be particularly attractive to my guests," Galwey reported with satisfaction when he had finished decorating his hut, adding with a little flourish, "most of whom have forgotten the appearance of the female form divine."[33] Just eighteen years old that winter, Galwey had already served in the army for more than two years—one wonders how much experience the young man had had with real women when he complained of "gaunt, half-starved natives" in Virginia, preferring instead the "more attractive" paper women he clipped from *Godey's* and *Leslie's* upon whom he and "the boys can feast their eyes."³⁴

Cold and homesick, Galwey and his "boys" were comforted by the fashion plates as they gathered to ring in the new year; perhaps even Anthony Comstock would not have begrudged Galwey the images he preferred to hang on his walls. They seem to have been very different from the "obscene prints and photographs" that Tousley complained of in Tennessee. But in each case, the open/public display of women's bodies encouraged fraternity among the men, with the images serving as unspoken communication between them of emotions barely acknowledged—homesickness, of course, but also desire.

Sharing of erotic images between men served to negotiate lines of authority and trust. Colonel Peirce read from *Fanny Hill* to officers and enlisted men who had shown him little respect—the former admitted to regularly coughing loudly during drills, for instance—in an unsuccessful attempt to earn their favor. Captain Tousley described displays of erotic images that cut across rank and that he felt were negatively affecting his command of the regiment. A low-ranking officer, and a young man, Thomas Galwey wanted to entertain "the boys," and perhaps to impress them, when he purchased ladies' fashion monthlies and cut out pictures of "more attractive" women. And Lieutenant Lyman's cartes de visite were part of what seemed to be his overall flouting of military discipline, a condition that was aggravated by the regiment's close proximity to the main suppliers of pornography—not to mention women, with whom he and others had some familiarity. None of these men found himself in trouble with military authorities for having or sharing pornography; indeed, pornography served as a form of transaction among men who needed to know they could trust one another. But once the men were on trial, the porn was called to testify as a way of proving a soldier's unfitness and of meting out military discipline. Among the men on trial and those serving on military courts, there was widespread knowledge of and tolerance for the circulation of obscene materials in the U.S. Army, as long as the man in question met the expectations of his superiors and even, at times, those he commanded. These expectations generally corresponded with military code, but sometimes they were also grounded in the sexual culture of the U.S. Army camp, where men demanded access to one another's tents, a straight line of vision into sleeping quarters, and the right to watch one another and judge what they observed.

In U.S. Army camps, an expectation of privacy seemed to be a privilege of rank, but if court-martial proceedings are any indication, it was not one that other officers or enlisted men always respected. Three officers testified to untying the flaps on Lieutenant Lyman's tent, despite the best efforts of his assistant to prevent them, to see for themselves what they already knew—that Lyman was in bed with a woman. Sometimes the men came in groups.[35] When in April 1863 Major Lorenzo Phelps of the Fifth Regiment, West Virginia Volunteer Infantry, was court-martialed for conduct unbecoming—for drinking while on duty, contracting gonorrhea from a prostitute, and going AWOL—servants testified that Phelps beat his wife when she came to visit. Private William Pemberton testified that Phelps struck "her with his fist, and knock[ed] her down on the bed." When asked how he knew this, Pendleton responded, "I heard Maj. P. cursing in his room and looked through the key-hole."[36] According to Private Hugh Kerr, about twelve men observed Captain Hampden Waldron, Fifth Regiment, U.S. Veteran Volunteers, in camp in Providence, Rhode Island, on October 5, 1865, take "a woman of lewd character" into his quarters, where Waldron "did close the door, and draw down the window curtains." Kerr, whose quarters were adjacent to Waldron's, watched the couple make their way to the back room, through a hole in his door, which he described as "a small knot hole, about the size of a bullet."[37] Kerr's surveillance was no easy task, for the private described "lying on my belly with my eye to the hole."[38] Once the couple was out of site, Kerr continued his observation by putting his ear to the adjoining wall, where he heard the woman "give a sort of squeal like" and Waldron hush her.[39] In his defense, Waldron called Kerr a "skulking spy" and, somewhat disingenuously for a man who escorted a woman other than his wife into his quarters in the middle of the day, questioned Kerr's intentions in looking.[40] The court did not take the bait.

The voyeur was a stock character in early modern erotica—the observer who is posed just outside the frame, watching the sexual act in progress. If the image was intended as a criticism, the voyeur was rarely the target; indeed, the reader's expected reactions were often those expressed by the secret observer. In the nineteenth century, authors created other means of reproducing the perspective of the voyeur, offering viewers access to the most private of spaces through a number of literary tropes, such as those employed in Paul de Kock's *The Adventures of a French Bedstead* and in *The Flea*, a book by an unknown author. Here readers were invited to see from the privileged position of a piece of bedroom furniture or through the eyes of a pest that hopped from bed to body. In her study of postwar Germany, historian Dagmar Herzog refers to soldiers' "pornographically schooled gaze," and this might be a useful way to think about the connection between the sharing of pornography and the expectation that one can at any moment assume the position of a bedside voyeur.[41] In U.S. Army camps during the Civil War, young men peered over one another's shoulders to look at women's bodies in books, on cartes de visite, and in pictures hung up or propped up in the corner of tents. Captain Waldron might dismiss Private Kerr as a skulking spy, but watching and being watched—through keyholes, under doors, through tent flaps—was part of the sexual culture of the camps, an exchange not unlike the sharing of erotica.

Expanded access to suggestive words, at times spoken, and images that could be touched and handled helped to foster a camp culture of exchange and visual access. New print technologies made

Fig. 15. A stereoscope offering three-dimensional viewing of photographs operated in Culpeper, Virginia. (Edwin Forbes, "The Showman in Camp," *Frank Leslie's Illustrated*, 1864)

exchange possible, and photography blurred the lines between seeing and touching. In a 1864 sketch by *Frank Leslie's* artist Edwin Forbes titled "The Showman in Camp" (fig. 15), identified as Culpeper, Virginia, men stand in a group and take turns looking into a stereoscope, an innovation that featured twin images of the same scene that, when viewed through the scope, gave the illusion of three-dimensionality, or what contemporaries described as "being *in* the picture."[42] Images intended for the stereoscope often portrayed travel scenes—from Europe or the American West, for example—but erotica entrepreneurs were quick to adopt the technology, producing images such as one in Lowry's collection of Civil War images, which captures a woman lifting her skirt to pull up her stockings (fig. 16). The Library of Congress description characterizes the scene in figure 15 as a "peep show," indicating that the men paid money to see suggestive images rather than nature scenes. Placing African American boys in the

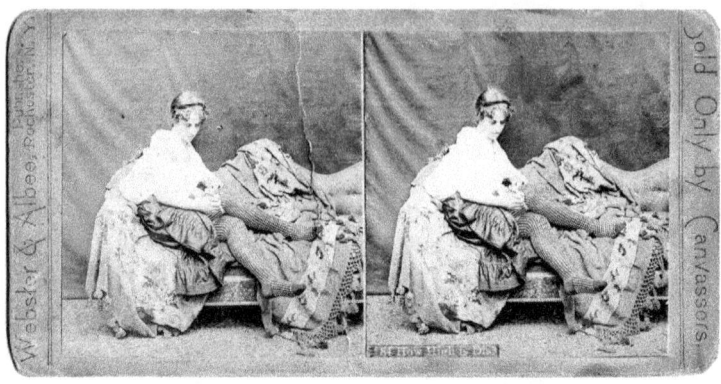

Fig. 16. Viewing twin photographs through a stereoscope gave viewers the feeling of being "in" the scene. ("How High Is Dis," stereoscopic photograph published by Webster & Albee, Rochester, New York, in the possession of Thomas Lowry; reprinted with permission)

sketch seems to have served little purpose other than to add to the lewd nature of the scene. With their head under the shade and their eyes trained on the eyepiece, soldiers placed themselves *in* the scene temporarily, where they could answer for themselves such questions as that posed at the bottom of figure 16: "How High is Dis?" Each man then stepped away from the scope, adjusted his eyes again to the sun, and yielded to the next in line. West of Richmond and Washington, D.C., Culpeper, like the handles of the stereoscope, changed hands repeatedly during the war, as one army retreated and another occupied. The showman's affiliation is unclear, but a show such as this might have piqued the interests and emptied the pockets of soldiers in both armies.

Peering through holes in doors and over one another's shoulders, privates and servants monitored the behaviors of their lieutenants, captains, and majors, denying them the privacy of rank and seeking through closed doors an unobstructed view to the intimate details of their lives. Pornography served as a means of social leveling, working against class and army hierarchy, as officers and enlisted men bonded over erotic images and words that explicitly violated the terms of domesticity and that could also embrace violence or domination. How men shared these images, expressions, touches, on the other hand, was a rejection of violence, a reaffirmation of fraternity.

Based on the idealized and private middle-class home, domesticity valued heterosociality, assumed women's sexual difference, and demanded male restraint. In the homosocial world of the army, Reid Mitchell showed, soldiers worried about the absence of women, commented on the occasional appearance of the wives of their commanders, and assumed "feminine" tasks of cooking, washing, and serving as dance partners to other men.[43] Engaged in a battle over the meaning of home, men sought to re-create in camp the relationships they enjoyed at home, and they did this, Mitchell found, by finding surrogates in other men. We might interpret cutout images from magazines, suggestive playing cards, and cartes de visite as evidence of what Mitchell found to be northern soldiers' deep ties to home, but these things also marked the physical and sensual distance from it. Women portrayed in fashion prints or period pornography, like the female nurse or the captain's wife, were remote and unattainable. Rather than disrupting the homosocial world of the camp, paper women and pornography helped to sustain it. They formed part of a sexual culture composed of a constellation of obscene words and images, ways of seeing and touching, through which men negotiated authority and trust. Women were removed from this world twice over—once due to their absence and again in their appearance as characters in erotic books and images.

When Colonel Peirce was found guilty of, among other things, conduct unbecoming an officer and a gentleman, his peers who sat on the military court sentenced him to dismissal. At the last minute, his command was restored to him, and Peirce was in command of the Twenty-Ninth Massachusetts at White Oak Swamp, Virginia, in June when a cannonball struck him and tore off his right arm. Having narrowly survived the court-martial proceedings, the loss of his right arm proved harder to endure. Peirce continued to serve for two years after he was injured, but in November 1864 Peirce, now a brigadier general, was discharged for disability and "due to the general nervous debility resulting from the miasmatic diseases."[44] Peirce lived to be eighty, but like others who served in the Peninsula Campaign, he never fully regained his health. Although injured and at times ill, Peirce nonetheless appeared to prefer camp life. Having served in the Massachusetts militia before the war, he returned to his post after he left the U.S. Army. Sometime between 1870 and 1880, Ebenezer Peirce and Irene, his wife of some twenty years, divorced; perhaps his illness proved too much for her, or maybe she had had enough of being a soldier's wife. Perhaps the behaviors—adultery, misplaced violence, and an appetite for pornography—we catch a glimpse of in the 1862 court-martial proceedings reveal a pattern of behavior that ill-fitted Peirce for middle-class domesticity. Or maybe the couple that had spent considerable time apart could not imagine living together. In her study of life in the Gold Rush camps, Susan Johnson explores "a crisis of representation" in which white miners wondered how they would "make sense—for themselves, for each other, and for folks back home—of what they did find and see and touch in the diggings."[45] Of course, U.S. Army soldiers did not write home about what they saw on the battlefield any more than what they read in obscene books, saw through the stereoscope, or gazed at through the keyhole; some may have found themselves facing a crisis of their own, about how to make sense to themselves and others of the sexual culture of the camp and how they engaged it.

THREE

TRUE COURAGE

Anthony Comstock and the Crisis of the War

The *New Haven Columbian Register* carried the news on July 11, 1863 — ten days after the Seventeenth Connecticut sustained heavy losses at Barlow's Knoll on the first day of the Battle of Gettysburg. "The 17th Connecticut went into the fight with 17 officers and 369 men," the story read, "and came out with 10 officers and 21 men."[1] Part of the Eleventh Corps, the Seventeenth was hit hard that first day; the men who remained retreated up Cemetery Hill, continuing the fight until the three-day battle was over. The Seventeenth left Gettysburg on July 6 in pursuit of the Army of Northern Virginia, and when they did they left behind, among many other wounded men, twenty-one-year-old Samuel Comstock of New Canaan, Connecticut. The newspaper account reported that he had been wounded and taken prisoner, but by the time his family read it Samuel was at one of the many hospitals in the war-ravaged town. Samuel engaged in and was witness to war's brutality; at Chancellorsville, when the regiment lost half its number, and then again at Gettysburg, he participated in the killing and saw his friends and comrades killed all around him.[2] Suffering a staggering ninety percent casualty rate, the seventeenth was practically wiped out in three days of fighting.

Samuel died in Gettysburg on September 27. His close friend and fellow townsman Justus Silliman accompanied his body back home to Connecticut and stood beside his grave as he was buried.[3] Violence tore the regiment apart, but it also drew the men together, building

Fig. 17. The Seventeenth Connecticut's service at the Battle of Gettysburg was recognized at the 1884 dedication of this monument. Although his brother Samuel died at Gettysburg, Anthony Comstock did not attend the dedication. (*Summit of Barlow's Knoll, Gettysburg*, 1900–1906, Detroit Publishing Company Photograph Collection, LC-DIG-det-4a11026 [digital file from original]; Prints and Photographs Division, Library of Congress)

strong bonds between them. Mustered in as a private, Samuel was buried a year later as a sergeant. In addition to a simple headstone at his Connecticut grave, Samuel's name and rank are included on the Seventeenth's monument at Gettysburg, dedicated in 1884 (fig. 17). Samuel's younger brother, Anthony Comstock, contributed to the monument fund, but he did not attend the reunion, when veterans gathered on Barlow's Knoll, where they had fought and where so many young men had lost their lives, including Sergeant Samuel Comstock. Wounded himself that day twenty years earlier, Justus Silliman was there to honor Samuel.[4]

Anthony Comstock mustered into the Seventeenth on December 30, 1863, three months nearly to the day after his brother Samuel died. Young Anthony was determined to take his brother's place. Some years later, Anthony explained his impulse to enlist to his official biographer. "The Comstock boys could not stay out of army life while there was a fight for principle waging," Anthony recalled. Though threatened with the loss of the family's heavily mortgaged farm if they enlisted, the Comstock boys "had learned to believe that some things are more valuable than others, and they preferred to lose a farm and hold on to honour and duty."[5] In richly gendered language, Anthony Comstock characterized his and Samuel's war service in terms associated with *manliness,* or those characteristics most valued by middle-class men; historian Gail Bederman has described these as "self-restraint, a powerful will, a strong character."[6] Whereas *duty* evoked the high morals associated with manliness, *honor* was something that men fiercely defended, with swords or fists, in violent rituals that were still strong among the elite in the South but that were increasingly associated with the rough working classes in the antebellum North.[7] Continuing the theme of honor, Comstock described his introduction to army life in the South Carolina sea islands as "severe," as "the men had to lie in a swamp" and huddle "close enough together to keep warm." He recalled the "sickening, sinking sensation of being under fire" with "the wounded increasing on every side." During those "perilous days," Comstock learned to conquer his fears, a characteristic of "true courage wherever it is found," his biographer concluded.[8] It is an old story, really: two brothers linked by a Civil War experience that tested their manhood, in which they fulfilled their duty and defended the honor of their family and their nation. One succumbed to the war's violence, and one managed to survive it.

Except that Anthony Comstock never experienced these things. His references to combat and danger—and the camaraderie and courage that got him through it—are a fiction, an imagined military career. Comstock, the moral crusader, created this story at the end of his life, as he looked back on a long career of fighting porn, or obscenity, as he called it. Part of a sedentary and inactive occupying force in St. Augustine, Florida, in the last year and half of the war, Comstock struggled to fill his days and nights. Deprived of the opportunity to experience real soldiering, to learn to stomach the violence, to exhibit courage, Comstock killed time. Coming of age in the army proved to be profoundly unsettling for him. He lived the Civil War's "crisis in gender" at a microhistorical level.[9]

Uncomfortable with the men around him and isolated and confused by his feelings, Comstock poured out his thoughts in a diary he kept as a soldier, fragments of which have survived. Using these fragments along with other evidence of his war service, this chapter seeks to understand how Anthony Comstock experienced the Civil War as a personal crisis, one that was aggravated, he thought, by what he saw, read, and felt. Having survived this internal battle between restraint and indulgence, in which he believed he had been a victim, he launched a new one of his own making. In Comstock's mind the two wars, the Civil War (the one he never fought in, the one that nearly defeated him) and the war against porn (the one from which he emerged bruised and scarred but nonetheless victorious), remained forever conflated. In the war of his own invention, Comstock aimed to save young men from their erotic imagination. But first, as we shall see, he had to save himself.

Connected to distinctions between private and public behavior, the terms "obscene" and "obscenity" have a much longer history than does "pornography." The Oxford English Dictionary traces two separate but interlocking uses of the first two terms. "Obscene" describes an "indecent [or] lewd" publication or something that offends "against moral principles" or is repugnant.[10] Words, images, and women were often described as obscene—as in lewd or indecent—but so too were deeds and excesses, particularly pecuniary. "Obscenity" was determined by community expectations and values, but in the mid nineteenth-century "pornography" emerged as a creature of the courts. "Something shifted in the balance between obscenity and decency, private and public, and porn emerged as a distinct governmental concern," Lynn Hunt has explained.[11] Anthony Comstock used the term "obscene" to describe the newspapers, dime novels, and cartes de visite he confiscated, but his approach and his intentions were aligned with the pornography project that took place in courtrooms.

As described in the court cases in chapter 1, pornography was defined, in courtrooms, as something produced with the intention to corrupt "young minds."[12] Antebellum prosecutors and postbellum reformers invoked the "young person" to move local officials to enforce laws and strengthen them. In the British and French contexts, this "young person" was often a young and naïve maiden. In the case *Regina v. Hicklin*, British justices ruled as obscene a publication that "would suggest to the minds of the young of either sex, or even to persons of more advanced years, thoughts of a most impure and libidinous character."[13] These concerns were so well known that Charles Dickens poked fun at them in his 1864–65 novel, *Our Mutual Friend*. In the book, Georgina Podsnap narrowly avoids seduction, and her father, Mr. Podsnap, the comic character, remains exercised about protecting his daughter, although she is eighteen years old and rather world-wise. "A certain institution in Mr. Podsnap's mind which he called 'the young person,'" Dickens explained, "may be considered to have been embodied in Miss Podsnap, his daughter. It was an inconvenient and exacting institution, as requiring everything in the universe to be filed down and fitted to it." Dickens coined the term "Podsnappery" to capture this overwrought concern for the "young person," who existed in the minds and mouths of moral reformers.[14] An American Mr. Podsnap, Anthony Comstock spent decades hunting down men who intended to corrupt "the Young Person," except for Comstock the "young person" was always a boy. Comstock's campaign marks the moment that Americans became alerted to the problem of pornography, when pornography was linked in the American imagination with boys and young men.

The history of pornography and antipornography in the United

States begins at the moment of crisis ushered in by war, when what it meant to be a man and how boys should go about becoming men were openly and heatedly debated. Clashes and disagreements over these concerns predated the Civil War. Fissures ran through the understanding of and adjudication of military discipline, and they became part of the way the war generation remembered the war — Anthony Comstock's imagined Civil War, for example. Private Anthony Comstock, Company H, Seventeenth Connecticut, U.S. Volunteers, was the "young person" threatened.

Courage was a central concern among men who fought in the war. Historian Gerald Linderman found that among Civil War soldiers the terms "courage" and "manhood" were used interchangeably, and the key moment to prove one's courage came in battle. "Courage," writes Linderman, "served as the goad and guide of men in battle."[15] Soldiers looked forward to combat because it offered them the opportunity to exhibit courage, and they fretted when circumstances such as illness kept them from it. Charles Harvey Brewster, Tenth Regiment, Massachusetts Volunteers, obsessed about missed opportunities to prove his courage and manhood. In the Peninsula Campaign in spring 1862, Brewster suffered from severe diarrhea that left him "reduced [to] hardly anything but skin and bones," but he would not come home, for "the brave ones that staid at home would call me coward and all that so I must stay here until after the fight."[16] Concerns about "courage" effeminating were echoed in worries expressed by soldiers who missed combat and who remained eager to prove their courage.

Reading figured prominently into antebellum conversations about manliness, with advocates of physical culture cautioning against sedentary pastimes and others emphasizing making proper reading choices.[17] Antebellum doctor and educator William Alcott compared choosing books to choosing friends and encouraged young men to find a debating society or lyceum circuit to be directed to "well selected" books and develop good reading habits. So strong were the effects of reading on young minds and bodies, Alcott offered guidelines for readers. It was better not to read too long or too much, nothing too exciting, and definitely not at night, for, he warned, "fancy and imagination are apt to predominate, at this hour of the day." Alcott strongly advised against "light reading" or anything meant to "'kill time.'" Instead, young men should seek "to make a wise and profitable use of their leisure hours."[18]

The language of waste and profitability tied injunctions against certain kinds of reading to concerns about masturbation as nonreproductive sex and to the emergent ethic of restraint.[19] What, how, and when one read—like other uses of leisure time—was tied up in aspirations for middle-class manliness. Prescriptive texts warned loudly and often against reading sentimental fiction, indicating that antebellum Americans generally ignored this advice and read novels voraciously and promiscuously. Injunctions against wasteful reading responded to the explosion of novels and other sorts of "light reading," but they did not reflect the reality that antebellum Americans read, as historian David Stewart has explained, because it was precisely nonproductive, not work.[20] Reading urban crime novels, pornography, and other "evil books" offered a release from the regimented workplace not unlike that recommended by advocates of physical culture. Health advocates and moral reformers shared a degree of ambivalence about reading and what it said about the man. The author of the *United States Service Magazine* article "Ethics and Humanities of War" insisted that military discipline and the active life would restore manhood to the nation's "dyspeptic youth."[21] While the army did not allocate resources or time to thinking about leisure pursuits or what men would do in winter quarters, on the ground reading, playing cards, and other leisure activities became a point of contention between men who found themselves with time to kill and different understandings of what it meant to be a man.

Born into a middle-class family in decline, Anthony Comstock faced an uncertain future before the war. His father lost the family's heavily mortgaged farm at the beginning of the war and then disappeared, leaving his children to sort out the family's finances.[22] (Comstock's mother died when he was young.) Military service might have offered Anthony a path to middle-class manliness by strengthening his powers of restraint or offering him the vigorous companionship of men engaged in active military service. What he found was an experience that confounded his gender and class aspirations. Instead of rewarding restraint and hard work, soldiering relied on instinct and often on luck. And beyond the *work* of soldiering, there was a good deal of *leisure*. How they came to spend their leisure had profound explanatory power for men with strong class aspirations, like Anthony Comstock, and those who situated leisure within the heterosocial home; these men found the military camp a bewildering place with a mystifying set of expectations.[23] Like the men around him, Comstock found the idea of army life exhilarating and full of possibility, but companionship proved elusive, and the road to middle-class respectability, long. For a young man determined to achieve the self-mastery he associated with manliness, Comstock's nineteen months of service in the U.S. Army during the Civil War proved a great opportunity and a considerable challenge.

Comstock joined the ranks of the Seventeenth as the men underwent the transition from active service to a stationary post as an army of occupiers. Justus Silliman noted Anthony Comstock's arrival at camp in St. Augustine, but the younger brother of his friend Samuel did not figure prominently in Silliman's letters or the recollections of the other members of the Seventeenth. St. Augustine would seem to have been an ideal detail for army men who had seen active service in the first half of the war. An isolated outpost on the Atlantic, the town had briefly served as a Confederate fort before it was abandoned. The U.S. Army moved in, and the men made themselves comfortable amidst the largely Unionist townspeople. Here the men were supposed to defend the town if it was attacked by the Confederates, but beyond run-ins with a small Confederate cavalry unit nearby, the town needed no defending. By the time the Seventeenth Connecticut arrived, the men were asked to do little beyond drill and report for guard duty. The enlisted men enjoyed free access to the town when they were off duty. "I believe they all intend to be less rigid than heretofore," Silliman said of the Seventeenth's officers, and they "let us enjoy ourselves so long as we acted decently."[24] The men sailed, canoed, and fished in the bay and did not seem to regret their absence from active duty.[25] Silliman described the men of the Seventh Connecticut who shipped out as the Seventeenth arrived as "glum at [the] prospect of going to Virginia."[26] So relaxed was discipline among the Seventeenth that the men at times forgot that they were enemy occupiers, as when Colonel William Noble, Commander of the Seventeenth, was taken prisoner while riding, unarmed, in a carriage, and a few weeks later when several of his men were captured while at a dance twelve miles from camp, held by a local woman with suspect loyalties.[27] Even though his letters traced the ill effects on the regiment of too much leisure, Silliman, having seen hard service and survived injury, expressed no concern about missing combat, his own courage proven.

Although young and inexperienced, Private Anthony Comstock wasted no time testing the authority that came with his U.S. Army uniform. On January 25, just a few weeks after mustering in, Comstock reported in his diary that he "tried drilling company for first time" and began studying "a book of tactics."[28] "I resolved to know all that I can about Military life while in the Army," Comstock reported a few weeks later, having decided to fill his free time becoming a better soldier.[29] Comstock's studying paid off, he noted, when at inspection an officer pronounced his gun "the best cleaned" among the privates in Company H.[30] His early enthusiasm did not endear him to his comrades, however, and by March he reported that "Charlie became offended at me and threatened to leave my tent because I worked to [sic] hard."[31] The seasoned men and the new arrivals among the Seventeenth seem to have rather quickly sized up Anthony Comstock as an overeager green recruit, for a few days later Anthony admitted that he "heard some persons speaking against me."[32] By April he complained in his diary that men in his company used "unpleasant words" against him, and in May he noted a "conflict with feelings" with a fellow soldiers. By December Comstock's isolation was complete when he moved to his own quarters, only to return to his room to find "all the windows closed tight, room full of smoke. Bunk ful of rubbish and loaded with broken Benches, Chairs etc."[33] The incident highlights the tension between new recruits and veterans, particularly within hard-worn regiments like the Seventeenth. Although he dismissed the episode as an initiation, Comstock had been with the regiment for nearly a year when his comrades dumped trash on his bed. Pranks and practical jokes were part of the culture of rough manhood in the North, historian Richard Stott has shown, in which the honor of the victim was tested. To reclaim his honor, the victim retaliated; otherwise he was a "bad sport" and had no honor.[34] Surviving evidence suggests that Comstock did not retaliate.[35] He had resolved to learn all he could about "Military life" — even writing for materials to enroll in "Military School" — but military life confounded Comstock, and he had not endeared himself to his comrades.[36]

Beyond his preference for reading military tactics and his eagerness for playing the soldier, Comstock refused to participate in the culture of the camp — or, as he described it, "join with them in sin and wickedness."[37] With little power to enforce the discipline that he found lacking, he could only complain to his diary that the officers seemed uninterested in policing how the men of the Seventeenth spent their leisure time. And although he knew that he was losing "all of their friendship" in the process, after months of service Comstock could not have been surprised that he found himself alone. Indeed, many years later he would describe with relish his rejection of the "camp-fire comradeship" that came with drinking and smoking.[38] At the time, though, he preferred to read *their* rejection of *him* as a rejection of God. "Would that One of our Officers would stand on the Lord's side," he complained on April 24, 1864 — the same day that Justus Silliman wrote with relief that the officers were allowing the men to spend their leisure as they wanted — when he tried to stop the men from using the church "ever[y] night for singing and pleasure."[39]

"O how blessed, to feel that God is with me," he wrote on May 18, 1864, "though men are not." And on the next day, he was "blessed to feel that God was with me. Though some of [sic] comrades were against me."[40]

Faith alone cannot explain Comstock's isolation, though, for he attended meeting along with others and surely found among attendees those who shared his concerns for the moral health of his fellow soldiers. Indeed, Justus Silliman described crowded pews and declared that the men "were having a blessed revival."[41] "There seems to be a great interest felt here by the whole force," Silliman explained. Six days later, Silliman was baptized at a church in Jacksonville, just north of St. Augustine.[42] Silliman's conversion might have resulted from his own battlefield injury and from having attended Samuel Comstock's death at Gettysburg, but the packed meeting houses he described in east Florida were consistent with revivals taking place elsewhere in the U.S. Army in the lead-up to the spring campaign.[43] Anthony Comstock believed that his potential army comrades rejected him because he found their leisure pursuits morally objectionable, but he also struggled with his own understandings of manhood.

Among the fragments of Anthony Comstock's diary that were reprinted (from the original that is no longer extant) in Heywood Broun and Margaret Leech's 1927 *Anthony Comstock, Roundsman of the Lord*, there are references to the young man's internal struggles with feelings and impulses that suggest another cause for his isolation and his decision to remember it as a rejection of "campfire comradeship": at times, Comstock became provoked at the slights he endured and worked to control his temper.[44] He described himself as "weak and sinful" when he became angry. Beyond controlling his temper, the young man also confided in his diary when he struggled to control his sexual urges. "On camp guard today," he recorded on a hot day in July, "very severely tempted, and led almost into the lion's mouth."[45] Undated references credited to Comstock's diary revisit the theme of a young man wrestling with temptation. "Again tempted and found wanting. Sin, sin. Oh how much peace and happiness is sacrificed on thy altar," Comstock confessed, on a day when he had more success; it "seemed as though Devil had full sway over me today, went right into temptation, and then . . . Jesus snatched it away out of my reach."[46] Other days sin or Satan won, as on the day he wrote, "O I deplore my sinful weak nature so much. If I could but live without sin, I should be the happiest soul living. . . . What a day will it be when that roaring Lion shall be bound and his wanderings cease."[47] When he was "tempted by Satan," he credited his victories to God and his failures to his own weakness.[48]

To his friend and hand-selected biographer Charles Gallaudet Trumbull, Comstock recalled temptations to which he had been subjected as a youth, but he did not explain them further. "While the boy's childhood days were chiefly filled with the things that make for good," Trumbull wrote in 1913, "vicious characters in school and on the farm . . . started memories and lines of temptation that are harder for him to overcome than anything that ever came into his life in later years."[49] While we cannot know the exact source of his discomfort, Comstock traced his problems with self-control to his adolescence spent in public schools and among hired farm hands. Health reformer Sylvester Graham blamed public schools for the problem of masturbation.[50] Historian Paul Fussell noted among young soldiers on the Western Front with experience in public schools the tendency to develop crushes, "passionate but non-physical," and their eager embrace of army life as a "wholly masculine way of life uncomplicated by Woman."[51] Whatever were the "lines of temptation" that Comstock struggled with, his brief service in the U.S. Army during the Civil War severely tested them. Fifty years after he confided to his diary about going to battle with a "roaring lion," and after decades of marriage, he still referred to temptation in the present tense. Living in a world of men proved too much for Comstock, and he experienced the war as a personal crisis in masculinity. Could he aspire to manliness if he lacked self-restraint, failing to control his anger and sexual urges? Without restraint, what marked him as a Christian among sinners? It is no wonder he invented a story about his time in the U.S. Army full of danger, duty, and honor, for the one he lived was something else entirely. Young Private Comstock struggled alone with impulses that threatened his notions of manhood, but he did so alongside others.

Another Connecticut soldier, John W. De Forest, wrestled openly in his letters home with notions of manhood, his own and the men with whom he served.[52] De Forest was commissioned as a captain in the Twelfth Connecticut, serving under General Benjamin Butler in Louisiana and Philip Sheridan in the 1864 Shenandoah Valley Campaign. An author before and after the war, De Forest relished the deprivations of army life, echoing the proponents of gymnasia and the active life who scorned sedentary pursuits as effeminate.[53] "What with starving, freezing, swamp fever, forced marches, and being shot," De Forest wrote his wife in October 1864 from the Shenandoah Valley, "war is glorious fun."[54] In the Shenandoah Valley the fighting was anything but fun, as Sheridan's forces engaged in a fierce back-and-forth with Jubal Early's troops, stopping short of Richmond. De Forest unsparingly described the deadly consequences of the war, like after the Battle of Winchester, in September 1864, when he noted "piles and lines of dead and wounded which could hardly be estimated at less than 1500 men."[55] An estimated five thousand Union soldiers were killed or wounded in one day—Confederate losses were likely more than three thousand.[56] De Forest experienced the war as periods of intense combat punctuated by brief periods of rest, during which he picked up some of his old pursuits as a man of leisure. During the siege of New Orleans in April of 1862, De Forest said of himself and his fellow officers in the Twelfth Connecticut, "We smoked and read novels, we yawned often and slept a great deal; anything to kill time."[57] Although he was quick to dismiss as unmanly privates who spent money on whisky, De Forest made no apologies for how and when he "killed time."

Second Lieutenant James Graham of the Eightieth Ohio Volunteer Infantry Regiment seized every opportunity for leisure and expressed no misgivings about how he or others spent it. Advancing on Vicksburg with Grant's army in March 1863, on Union gunboats and then on foot, Graham chafed at the grueling pace of the campaign and hoped that it would soon slow. The twenty-one-year-old snatched slivers of time to himself, between the demands of an active campaign and nightly reveries that included whiskey, card playing, and pranks. Graham consumed books as heartily as he did whisky and kept track of both in his diary. In a March 6, 1863, entry he tried to count how many glasses of ale and whisky he drank before he was unable to find his tent. On March 16, before playing "whisky poker" and pranking his fellow officers, he read *The Orphan Princess*, which disappointed him for lack of a plot.[58] "Nothing doing today," Graham recorded on March 29, so he finished reading another book.[59] On May 3, after marching all day, Graham noted that he "cam across part of a book today the whole of which I would like to get entitled 'Caroline of Brunswick.'" Closing in on the enemy in retreat, he hoped for some time to rest and read it.[60] While awaiting orders early the next morning Graham read the book, discovering in it "some of the most beautiful descriptions of sensual passion and amorous persons that I have ever read." "Ah! What a pity that the writer had not devoted his descriptive and imaginative powers to something more worthy of his or her talent," Graham noted, but he finished it nonetheless.[61] Graham was likely referring to *The Murdered Queen! Or, Caroline of Brunswick, a Diary of the Court of George IV, by a Lady of Rank*, published in 1838, a secret history of the tragic marriage of the Princess of Wales who was denied ascension to the crown for her adultery—an eighteenth-century Princess Diana story, told from Caroline's perspective.[62] Like *Fanny Hill* the book that Colonel Ebenezer Peirce read aloud to his men, as described in chapter 2, the *Murdered Queen* that Graham enjoyed that early Monday morning, awaiting orders outside of Vicksburg, was made up of a series of letters exchanged between the princess and a female confidante in which the former revealed her dreams and stories of seduction, intrigue, and of course, murder.

Lieutenant Graham enlisted as a private and mustered out four years later as first lieutenant. His taste for whisky and preference for reading lurid tales about the interior worlds of European princesses seems not to have concerned his superiors, nor did it interfere with his military advancement.[63] Key to Graham's success was his performance in battles in Tennessee and Mississippi, including of course the long and grueling siege of Vicksburg.[64] Grant's army won a key victory in in mid-May, after having marched some 180 miles and inflicted some 7,200 casualties on the Confederates; during that time, young Graham seized moments here and there to read (parts of) three books.[65] Graham and the other members of the Eightieth Ohio fought at Jackson on May 14 and then regrouped outside of Vicksburg, where, according to another veteran, "for 47 days and nights it was constantly under fire" from the town's Confederate defenders. The July 4 surrender of Vicksburg was a critical victory for Union war aims, but the spring campaign was costly—Confederates counted twenty thousand men killed and wounded, and the Union reported nearly eleven thousand.[66] That the young man was able to retain his interest in reading fiction speaks to his considerable fortitude; neither his commanding officers nor his men begrudged Graham his scant leisure, whether he spent it drinking whisky or reading books about "amorous persons," and if any one weighed in on his manhood, it likely was related to his performance on the battlefield.

Whereas active campaigns produced their own discipline, regimental order books attest to efforts to impose discipline on men not actively engaged in the war. Officers periodically issued orders laying out rules for proper dress, cleanliness and grooming, behavior at drill, and expectations on guard duty; they issued injunctions against drinking, gambling, patronizing prostitutes, and reading obscene books.[67] U.S. Army regulations prohibited many of these behaviors, but repeated orders threatening men who engaged in them indicate that regulations were routinely ignored. Amidst a tightening up of a number of regulations regarding furloughs, regulation dress, drilling exercises, and inspection, two officers in the Fifty-Sixth Massachusetts Volunteer Infantry issued General Order 29, ordering company commanders to search and destroy "all obscene books, pictures, and c." and threatening to "severely punish" men who brought them into camp at Readville, Massachusetts, or those who had the items in their possession.⁶⁸ Having spent the winter in camp in Massachusetts, where the men seemed to be enjoying easy access to mass-produced erotica, the veterans of the Fifty-Sixth deployed to Maryland in the spring, and perhaps their commanders breathed a sigh of relief that the men were now on the move. Whereas the unorganized leisure the men of the Fifty-Sixth experienced in the three or four months spent in winter quarters presented a disciplinary challenge to company commanders, for the Seventeenth Connecticut these challenges extended throughout the year spent in St. Augustine.

The Seventeenth's regimental and company order books fill out some of the context of Private Anthony Comstock's enlistment experience, a period in which he struggled to restrain his thoughts and actions amidst a general loosening of disciplinary rigor. In March 1864, when Comstock was beginning to feel isolated among his fellow recruits and the Seventeenth's veterans, two officers issued an order reminding the enlisted men of the basic U.S. Army protocol of saluting their superiors.⁶⁹ In May, Lieutenant Colonel A. H. Wilcoxson issued an injunction against the widespread use, among enlisted men and their officers, of "profane, and indecent language." "Expressions of profanity, or vulgarity, are entirely inconsistent with the character of the true Soldier," the order read, "and it is hoped that the public notice of a practice so discreditable to men, who have the honor of representing the morality of Connecticut, will cause it to be discontinued."⁷⁰ Officers sought to prohibit profanity when it was indicative of a general lapse in discipline.⁷¹ The Seventeenth Connecticut's order book records discipline meted out throughout the summer to men who straggled on marches, left camp without permission, sold their army uniforms to civilian merchants, and swiped watermelon from a civilian's garden. Amidst a rash of episodes of men sleeping on guard duty in the fall, five men were court-martialed for the offence.⁷² In December, Colonel William Noble issued new orders intended to keep the men from abusing the system of passes required to leave the fort perimeter, where they were found "visiting and hanging about drinking saloons, and in disorderly conduct."[73] Passes could not be issued to men for the latter purpose, and they had to be obtained from headquarters, company captains, or the provost marshal, for whom, as of November, Anthony Comstock worked as a clerk.[74] From this vantage point, Comstock sat alongside of officers empowered with authority to regulate how and where soldiers spent their leisure. As a private, he would have been well advised to keep his own opinions on the subject to himself; a clerk's job was to record the decisions of the officers in charge. That Comstock did not use the position to ingratiate himself to his comrades is suggested by the prank in which the men filled his room with smoke and dumped trash on his bed, one month after he began working for the provost marshal.[75] It was a prank in which his honor was tested by the rough manhood of his comrades—a test that he seems to have failed.

Facing a prolonged period of inactivity and a generalized lapse in discipline, the Seventeenth's officers ordered all company commanders to read the Articles of War to their men once a week.[76] Beyond Article 2, which recommended that "all officers and soldiers diligently attend divine services," the Articles provided little guidance to soldiers on the proper use of their leisure time, but there were injunctions about its misuse. Articles 41, 42, and 43 prohibited officers and soldiers from leaving camp without permission and sleeping anywhere but their assigned quarters. Article 29 prohibited sutlers from selling liquor, staying open late, or entertaining on Sundays.[77] Article 45 threatened to cashier any officer who was drunk on duty, whereas noncommissioned officers and soldiers would be sentenced to corporal punishment for the same offence. Article 3 prohibited the use of "any profane oath or execration," and for all of those other offenses not anticipated, Article 83 threatened dismissal for any officer found guilty of "conduct unbecoming an officer and a gentleman."[78] Amidst great difference of opinion about what constituted gentlemanly conduct, there was yet an expectation that *all* men in the ranks live up to the standard.[79] Officers legislated these standards through regimental- or company-level orders.

Having issued injunctions against soldiers' insolence, swearing, neglecting their duty, and drinking away their leisure hours, the officers of the Seventeenth Connecticut hoped to induce good order by enforcing cleanliness and hygiene, other markers of army discipline and manliness. In December, Colonel Noble issued an order instructing the men of the Seventeenth to trim their beards, clean their tents, and scrub their cooking and eating utensils and to spit tobacco only in spittoons. "The Colonel Commanding is determined that this Regiment, shall as heretofore, exhibit the perfection of police, and military life in camp and garrison, for which it, and the 'old 2nd Brigade' were distinguished," Noble opined, referring to the Seventeenth's heyday, fighting at Chancellorsville and Gettysburg, that had come and gone before Anthony Comstock joined.[80] Noble's nostalgia for the regiment's past distinction predicted the official account the colonel wrote in 1911, when he recalled how the men had mustered in weeks after Antietam, when the "hour was dark, and there was desperate need of soldiers in field." Featuring companies of men formed from every major town in Fairfield County, Noble recalled, the Seventeenth's "departure was a rare scene of patriotic devotion and affection at parting" where friends and family "braced their hearts to the parting by pledges to keep all right and bright at the firesides."[81] But just weeks after writing the 1864 order that he hoped would bring about some of the discipline that the Seventeenth had lost while at St. Augustine, Colonel Noble was taken captive while riding *unarmed* in a carriage on his way back to St. Augustine from Jacksonville. Taken to Andersonville as a prisoner of war, without having been able to put up a fight, it was an ignoble end to an otherwise successful military career and perhaps helps to explain why Noble preferred to remember the Seventeenth's early years of service rather than later.[82] Similarly, after the Sixteenth Connecticut's career came to a tragic end when the men surrendered and were taken to prison camps, historian Lesley Gordon found that survivors spent the rest of their lives constructing a story of courage that met postwar expectations of manhood.[83]

Anthony Comstock had no point of reference with which to compare his experience with that of men who enlisted earlier or those who found themselves in regiments on active duty. He read manuals, polished his gun, and hoped for a chance to do his duty, to exhibit courage. "A volunteer," the *Military Handbook, and Soldier's Manual of Information* explained, "should earnestly strive to obtain a place in those regiments or companies which reject all 'hard cases' and men of vicious habits."[84] Instead of choosing a regiment by the personal habits of the men in it, Anthony Comstock followed his brother into a regiment of men from whom he felt increasingly alienated, because of either their habits or his. Once there, he struggled with his feelings and impulses and was surrounded by confusing rules and little order. Between inspection, drills, and guard duty, the war left men with time to kill. Waiting for something to happen, for orders to be given, could be deeply unsettling. "The dull monotony of this inactive life is again upon us," Lieutenant Robert Taggart of the Thirty-Eighth Pennsylvania commented in his diary in April 1862, adding "so long as we keep moving the men are [in] better health and spirits but to do nothing but lie around camp with an occasional drill is a sever on the physical constitution and baneful to the morals."[85] During Anthony Comstock's enlistment, the Seventeenth Connecticut suffered the indiscipline that accompanied a long period of inactivity, and officers and seasoned veterans provided late joiners—like the young men court-martialed for sleeping on guard duty—with little supervision. Noble cultivated a comforting nostalgia for the killing fields of Chancellorsville and Gettysburg that helped him endure the monotony of killing time. Comstock could only play the soldier.

In 1883, the year before Samuel Comstock's name was inscribed onto a monument at Gettysburg, his younger brother Anthony's name was included on a monument of his own. *Traps for the Young* (fig. 18) is

THE MODERN NEWS STAND AND ITS RESULTS.

Fig. 18. An illustration in Anthony Comstock's *Traps for the Young* dramatizes the threat to young people from reading story papers and other dailies. Here the proprietor operates near a public school. While a young girl peers at the offerings in the center image, around the perimeter the ill effects of this reading are associated exclusively with boys, who are driven to lives of crime, including theft, arson, and murder. (Anthony Comstock, "The Modern News Stand and Its Results," *Traps for the Young*, 1883, frontispiece.)

Anthony Comstock's most ambitious attempt to trace the routes of violence in young men to obscene reading materials. The book is filled with accounts of good boys gone bad by reading bad books, newspapers, and magazines. In an attempt to keep up with the "toughs," young men with "respectable parents" read the "hurrah for hades" publications, developed a taste for it, and eventually turned into ne'er-do-wells, gamblers, brawlers, robbers, and murderers.[86] The stories boys read in newspapers and dime novels "render the imagination unclean, destroy domestic peace, desolate homes, cheapen women's virtue, and make foul-mouthed bullies, cheats, vagabonds, thieves, desperadoes, and libertines." Images, too, were dangerous, for "the hideous appearance at first shocks the pure mind," but upon a second look, "a mighty force from within is let loose. Passions that had slumbered or lain dormant are awakened, and the boy is forced over a precipice."[87] Like the dime novels he despised, *Traps for the Young* recounted stories of boys and young men perpetrating all sorts of acts of violence: getting in fist and knife fights and shooting unsuspecting proprietors, passersby, their parents, teachers, and one another.[88] *Traps* left the impression that New York and other cities were in the midst of a violent crime wave perpetrated by teenage boys. "'A great majority of the prisoners arraigned in this court for burglary and other serious crimes,'" Comstock quoted the assessment of a New York City judge, "'are young men between the ages of seventeen and twenty-five years.'"[89] When he spoke with the youthful offenders, sometimes they traced their downfall to "evil reading," but Comstock offered no further explanation or proof of the connection between bad books and violent behavior. "There is a good deal of monkey in a bad boy," he explained, as a way of pointing out what to him seemed obvious.[90]

Full of youthful villains, *Traps* featured a prominent victim who also served as the book's hero: Anthony Comstock. Books turn a child into a daydreamer, causing him to wander "in thought from all that is real and of highest importance."[91] "Spent part of day foolishly as I look back," Comstock had confessed to his diary in the fall of 1864, "read a Novel part through."[92] Then there were days when the young private, daydreaming perhaps, confessed to having been "led almost into the lion's mouth" while on guard duty at St. Augustine.[93] "To one thus beguiled in youth, the future has many sorrows," Comstock warned in *Traps for the Young*, with perhaps his own experience in mind.[94] Bad books led to bad company, Comstock explained in *Traps*, where "if one is asked to drink and refuses, he is set up and twitted till he yields or is compelled by force."[95] "Have been twitted several times today about being a Christian," the young enlistee had confided in his diary, just a few weeks after arriving in camp with the Seventeenth Connecticut.[96] Twenty years after his difficult and disappointing service in the U.S. Army, Comstock still wrestled with what it meant about him as a man. He did not attend the reunion that next year, when aging veterans converged on Gettysburg to unveil the monument to the men who died there in 1863. Doing so would have forced him to confront the truth behind "those perilous days," as he would later remember his war service, when he learned to conquer his fears, exhibit "true courage."[97] Having neither participated in nor acknowledged the real war, Comstock had an acute sense, nonetheless, that he had been one of its victims: he was the "Young Person" threatened.[98] In the all-male world of the military camp he had struggled with what he saw and felt, and afterward Comstock's imagination continued to dwell on young men, many of them the same age as the boys he had attended public school with, and some who likely reminded him of those with whom he had served.

Except that in this imaginary war Comstock got to be the hero. Appearing at the same time as the *Century Magazine* ran its popular series of war reminiscences written by hundreds of soldiers of all ranks, *Traps* is Comstock's own memoir. "Few have had the opportunity of seeing and knowing the facts concerning the evils discussed in this book," Comstock began *Traps for the Young*, warning readers that it was only after long exposure to these evils that the author had become immune.[99] It was a veteran's conceit to claim particular knowledge such as he did. So too was referring to one's scars, which Comstock was wont to do about one on his left cheek, "relic of one of the many attempts on his life," his biographer explained.[100] Deprived of the opportunity to experience real soldiering, Comstock told a story full of the danger and violence he suspected were part of that experience. During the war Comstock had wrestled with his ability to achieve restrained manhood, bothered by what he read, perhaps, and what he saw, but in his postwar self-portrait he embraced the new ethic of masculinity. "His Atlas shoulders of enormous breath and squareness, his chest of prodigious girth, surmounted by a bull-like neck," as his biographer described his sixty-nine-year-old subject, "are in keeping with a biceps and a calf of exceptional size and iron solidarity."[101] Comstock was a fighter, with a fighter's build. Casting around for one more war reference to make the point, however, Comstock came up with an analogy more accurate than battle.

"When on picket duty in the army he had learned to accept assignments of unpleasant duty," Trumbull explained, "and to stay by them until relieved."[102] Of course, Anthony Comstock knew a good deal about standing guard; in the army it had been his main occupation, his only experience of war. And, as Trumbull put it, he was still waiting to be relieved.

FOUR

OUTRAGED MANHOOD OF OUR AGE

The Postwar Antipornography Campaign

The second session of the Thirty-Eighth Congress began on December 5, 1864, with another round of deliberations on the proposed Thirteenth Amendment. The Senate voted in favor of the amendment in April, but the House voted it down in June. The amendment was in front of the House again at the opening of the new session, bolstered now by Lincoln's reelection. In January, House debates on the amendment were stalled by rumors of a potential negotiated peace and then again by last-minute proposals to make emancipation gradual and compensated. On January 31 congressmen voted for emancipation—immediate, uncompensated, and final. Two weeks later, Henry Highland Garnet became the first African American to speak in the House chamber when he complimented congressmen on their latest effort and pushed them to do more.[1] The Thirteenth Amendment marked the first of three important pieces of legislation produced by the Thirty-Eighth Congress focused on emancipation and what would come next for freed people.

Late in February, congressmen passed S.R. 82, an act to "encourage enlistments and to promote the efficiency of the military forces of the United States." While the Thirteenth Amendment went to the states for ratification, this lesser known measure extended the immediate reach of emancipation by freeing "soldier wives and children owned by masters in the loyal border states exempt from the 1863 Emancipation Proclamation."[2] As historian Amy Dru Stanley has shown, the measure, initiated by abolitionist senators concerned about reports of slave masters abusing the wives of enlisted men, was both practical and humanitarian. The measure proposed freeing enslaved wives as compensation to their enlisted husbands. Senators debated the Thirteenth Amendment alongside S.R. 82, and the outcome of both measures turned on how members of the Thirty-Eighth Congress defined marriage. The wording of S.R. 82 traces the contours of the extraordinary debate that gripped congressmen for months as they tried to define marriage among slaves. "In determining who is or was the wife," the act explained, lawmakers defined "sufficient proof" as "evidence that he and the woman claimed to be his wife have cohabitated together, or associated as husband and wife," or "evidence that a form or ceremony of marriage ... has been entered into or celebrated by them." Senators raised questions about what effect such measures might have on the institution of marriage. One senator asked, in response to an early proposal that the Thirteenth Amendment declare a universal freedom, "I suppose before the law a woman would be equal to a man, a woman would be as free as a man. A wife would be equal to her husband and as free as her husband before the law."[3] The senator's question was rhetorical—and his fears became irrelevant, in any case, with the more conservative wording of the amendment—but concerns about upsetting the relationship between husband and wife lie just below the surface of debates about slave emancipation. "The heart of the matter," Stanley explains, "was the sovereignty that would supplant the slave master's."[4] Again and again, congressmen invoked the institution of marriage in debates about emancipation, and in the end they passed laws that affirmed that sovereignty would remain with the husband.

Then, on the last day of the session, congressmen voted to create the Freedmen's Bureau. Among the duties taken up by agents of this new federal agency was an ambitious effort to regularize marriage practices among freed women and men. Examining Freedmen's Bureau reports and war widow pension applications, historian Katherine Franke found that, rather than universally enjoying the "freedom to marry," many freedmen were forcibly "inducted into the regulatory regime of marriage" by rigorous enforcement of local antibigamy and antifornication laws. Franke sees something else at work, beyond humanitarian relief. With "the integrity of white male agency" no longer opposed to slavery, "white masculinity required new ground on which to be set off."[5] That ground was marriage. Early in 1865, as members of the Thirty-Eighth Congress debated various measures that would give shape to the postwar, postemancipation nation, their thoughts turned from the battlefields, freedmen's villages, and contraband camps where emancipation was being made on the ground to their own homes as they wondered what, if any, effects would be felt there. Would marriage survive the war, they wondered? Would it be the same?

The anxieties that drove Anthony Comstock to question his manhood and to disparage that of those around him were not unlike concerns expressed by congressmen who worried about how to preserve the sovereignty of husbands over wives, fathers over children, even as they sought to dissolve that of masters over slaves. Comstock experienced a deeply personal crisis in masculinity during his time in the U.S. Army, while some members of the Thirty-Eighth Congress remained concerned about retaining the prerogatives of one inequality while legislating away another. In this context, it is not entirely surprising that, in the midst of debating the provisions of a mundane post office bill, lawmakers' thoughts turned once again to relationships of a more intimate manner. The 1865 federal antipornography law was passed as a war measure, but it also marked the beginning of a postwar surge of interest in and legislation regularizing and regulating marriage and, in so doing, stabilizing a gender order that the war had upset. Antiabortion laws were part of that effort.

Early in February, shortly after senators completed their work on S.R. 82 and little more than a week after the Thirteenth Amendment's narrow victory in the House, senators briefly discussed an amendment to Senate Bill 390, An Act Relating to the Postal Laws, a measure that would prohibit the mailing of obscene materials through the U.S. Mail. The amendment read:

> And be it further enacted, That no obscene book, pamphlet, picture, print or other publication of a vulgar and indecent character, shall be admitted into the mails of the United States; but all such obscene publications deposited in or received at any post office, or discovered in the mails, shall be seized and destroyed, or otherwise disposed of, as the Postmaster General shall direct. And any person or persons who shall deposit or cause to be deposited in any post office or branch post office of the United States, for mailing or for delivery, an obscene book, pamphlet, picture, print, or other publication, knowing the same to be of a vulgar and indecent character, shall be deemed guilty of a misdemeanor, and, being duly convicted thereof, shall, for every such offence, be fined not more than $500, or imprisoned not more than one year, or both, according the circumstances and aggravations of the offence.[6]

Vermont senator Jacob Collamer, chairman of the Committee on the Post Office and Post Roads, introduced the amendment, apologizing to his fellow senators in the event they were not "perhaps entirely satisfied with it" but nonetheless entreating them to take the matter seriously as it aimed at protecting the soldiers, for "our mails are made the vehicle for the conveyance of great numbers and quantities of obscene books and pictures, which are sent to the Army, and sent here and there and everywhere, and this is getting to be a very great evil."[7] Ohio senator John Sherman, brother of William Tecumseh Sherman, endorsed the measure, saying, "We are all well aware that many of these publications are sent all over the country from the city of New York." Because they were familiar with the obscene items being discussed and the threat they posed, no one elaborated on these points. Indeed, Senator Sherman believed the problem so obvious and erotic publications so recognizable that he saw no reason to empower postmasters to seize these items and proposed striking out that clause, arguing that the threat to prosecute those who placed items in the mail would be sufficient deterrent. Maryland senator Reverdy Johnson added that he thought seizing and destroying mail set a dangerous precedent, and in any case, "after the postmaster takes the material out, what is he to do with it? May he circulate it if he thinks proper?"[8]

Johnson, a Democrat, was alone in pushing senators to define what they meant by "obscene," asking if it were not possible that the prohibition might be used to censor political speech and invoking memories of the congressional gag rules that were used against abolitionists. Despite Johnson's dissent, senators left the matter of definition unresolved. They closed ranks, however, in their concern to avoid dangerous precedent, striking the line, "but all such obscene publications deposited in or received at any post office, or discovered in the mails, shall be seized and destroyed, or otherwise disposed of, as the Postmaster General shall direct." The House, in the meantime, was resolving several different versions of H.R. 51 that would create the Freedmen's Bureau but nonetheless endorsed the new antiporn measure, with no debate, on February 21.[9] In a session in which federal lawmakers had engaged in protracted debates about marriage — how to define, protect, and enforce it — slipping an antiporn measure into an omnibus post office law was not a detour but, rather, another expression of their effort to shape domestic relations in the postwar nation. Although congressmen had not explicitly granted postmasters the power to destroy obscene publications directed to soldiers at the front — or "here and there and everywhere" — federal employees now had a powerful law at their disposal to control what went into the mail.

The matter-of-fact way in which senators discussed the proposal belied Collamer's reservations about how they would receive it. Senators were aware of the problem, and they believed they ought to do something about it. No doubt, some had come across the stuff themselves, or perhaps they had heard from soldiers about the availability of erotica in army camps. Congressmen with sons serving—Senator Lyman Trumbull, for instance, or James Dixon, William Fessenden, Jacob Howard, John C. Ten Eyck, Ira Harris, or Edgar Cowan—had opportunity to become aware of the situation in camp and, perhaps, to endorse the measure based on these intimate connections.[10] And, of course, complaints about the wide availability of porn in U.S. Army camps had periodically made their way into newspapers. "Postmasters in all directions complain that the mails are extensively prostituted to immoral and vicious purposes," read a complaint printed in the *Centinel of Freedom*, published in New Jersey, Senator Ten Eyck's home state, "and that through this channel obscene books, circulars, &c., are sown broadcast [sic] throughout the country."[11]

Precedent was an important consideration, but so too was popular will and public interest. Of the latter, though, there seemed to be little. The 1865 law yielded only a smattering of arrests and no public commentary. Records indicate that authorities arrested Benjamin Day under the federal law in 1865 for "mailing obscene pictures," but no further information could be found about the matter. Day's newspaper, the *New York Sun*, had been criticized for its coverage, sometimes in lurid detail, of the murder of Helen Jewett in 1836. By the time of his arrest, though, the publisher had been retired for decades.[12] Day was released after posting bail. What, if anything, to make of this first arrest under federal antipornography law remains unclear; the same can be said about the next three arrests, made between 1866 and 1868. The fate of "P. A. Stuart, citizen," arrested for "circulating obscene books & c. through the mails," is unclear in the records. Authorities arrested S. B. Alrich, who appeared under an alias as "Dr. S. Batcheldor," for "circulating obscene books & c. through the mails," but he jumped bail and was never found. The federal attempt to weed out pornography from the U.S. Mail had no teeth. As the soldiers came home, concerns about what they were reading escaped the realm of federal enforcement, becoming a problem, instead, for local communities.

New York passed an antiobscenity law on April 24, 1868, riding the beginning of a wave of interest in such measures. News of the law shared space in the local papers with updates on Andrew Johnson's impeachment trial. The *New York Times* covered the debate under "Minor Topics," comparing the public's interest in "light and flashy reading" to sex and dismissing its prohibition as doomed to failure.[13] Sponsored by the New York Young Men's Christian Association (YMCA), the new law passed along strictly party lines, with the Democrats arguing that the effort was simple censorship of the Democratic press, a claim that was not refuted by the *New York Tribune*.[14] "The suppression of obscene, immoral, and disgusting literature," the *Tribune* effused, "would strike out of existence half of the Democratic journals in the country."[15] The paper championed the law as a triumph and just punishment for newspapers that had fueled copperheadism during the war. This had been precisely Senator Reverdy Johnson's point when he likened the federal measure to the antiabolition gag rules. Johnson's home state of Maryland passed a similar measure a month earlier.[16]

New York's new prohibition significantly expanded the reach of the law, outlawing not only the sale but also the possession of "any obscene and indecent book, pamphlet, paper, drawing, painting, lithograph, engraving, daguerreotype, photography, stereoscopic picture, model, cast, instrument or article of indecent or immoral use."[17] The long list of obscene items now prohibited by New York state law indicates how the trade had expanded beyond the "yellow-covered" books that had concerned antebellum reformers. One could now find erotica in a great variety of forms, including photographs and the three-dimensional stereoscopic. And, beyond the street corner dealer, pornography was now transmitted through many more channels, all explicitly prohibited by the new law; dealers were forbidden to deposit items at "any post office within this State," express company, or "any common carrier" or include them in "any circular, handbill, card, advertisement, book, pamphlet or notice." New York's antiporn law defined as illegal the receipt of the prohibited items and, significantly, offered a cash reward to "the informer upon whose evidence the person so offending shall be convicted." This "informer" was to be awarded a third of the fine collected upon conviction. The law empowered postal officials and a variety of others who came in contact with the stuff to define it as obscene; indeed it offered an attractive incentive.[18]

Whereas federal lawmakers, concerned to avoid a negative precedent, had left out a confiscation order, New York state congressmen directed the police, upon receipt of a complaint, to "seize and take possession of such obscene and indecent books, papers, articles and things" and to then "transmit, enclosed and under seal, specimens thereof to the District Attorney" and deposit the remainder "under seal," "within the county jail of his county or such other secure place," until a conviction was attained, at which point the incarcerated items were to be destroyed. Repetition of the directive, "under seal," underscored that state officials felt that they were dealing with highly infectious material—porn had the power to corrupt any and all who came in contact with it. Previous measures had proven ineffective in containing it; indeed, they had failed, even, to see obscenity in all its many forms. Among the items now prohibited under New York state law was any "article or medicine for the prevention of conception or procuring an abortion."[19]

The linking of pornography and abortion began in this postwar moment. Added as riders on or amendments to measures seeking to combat obscene publications, prostitution, and other postwar ills, antiabortion laws were passed by doctor-veterans interested in driving irregular medical practitioners out of business. State lawmakers took them up, gingerly at times, as they spoke to concerns about marriage and domestic relations. By historian James Mohr's count, from 1866 to 1877 legislatures passed more than thirty such measures in states throughout the country, including those undergoing Reconstruction under Republican rule.[20] Maryland's earlier injunction was attached to a bill on professionalizing medicine and provided incentives to "informers." When state lawmakers revised it the next year, only the antiabortion statute was left.[21] New York's law took inspiration from Maryland's, except that it tied pornography closely to abortion, setting a precedent that would be followed closely by other states.

Doctors took advantage of the absence of a definition of obscene to target a range of unlicensed medical providers. Building on a growing sense that obscene materials were a threat, proponents of these laws, like federal lawmakers, saw obscenity "here and there and everywhere," including in the birth control and abortion services provided by midwives, homeopaths, and others whose practices were outside of the reach of profession-conscious doctors. And, like U.S. congressmen, state lawmakers were convinced that marriage was at risk. Whereas in enacting antipornography measures legislators echoed concerns by army whistle-blowers and reformers about the effect of obscene words and images on the "young person," the link between abortion and marriage remained unarticulated in this early legislation.[22] In debate, Ohio senator L. D. Griswold insisted that abortion threatened the sanctity of marriage and tried to have that concern written into the law that Ohio legislators passed in 1867.[23] Pornography came to be associated in lawmakers' minds and in state law with other perceived ills, such as prostitution, abortion, and birth control. Physicians who tried and failed—as they did in Maryland—to promote these laws based on their own professional interests succeeded in doing so by associating them with a vague but growing anxiety about obscenity, a concern that had compelled federal congressmen to act in 1865 and that now received a sympathetic hearing in statehouses, where legislators were again hard-pressed to define it but were nonetheless convinced they should prohibit it. As in federal emancipation debates, state lawmakers admitted to a faint but gnawing sense that marriage was at stake. If the war and its attendant disruptions had fatally undermined marriage, then legislating against pornography and associated obscenities was part of the solution.

Early measures outlawing pornography and abortion advertisements were part of a multipronged legislative response to what some believed was a marital crisis. Religious and secular commentators filled the newspapers with alarm and dark predictions for the future of traditional marriage. The *New York Times* published a series of editorials about easy access to divorce that one commentator likened to "a disease that is undermining family life." Without hard data, commentators nonetheless asked, "Is it true that divorces are increasing?" and wondered whether Americans divorced more readily than Europeans.[24] The federal government renewed its war against Mormon polygamy, or slavery's "twin relic of barbarism," with a series of coercive measures, including one that threatened to suspend Mormon men's citizenship rights.[25] States followed suit in enforcing marriage conformity by enacting antimiscegenation laws outlawing interracial marriage and, in so doing, "locating the production of race in the institution of marriage."[26] Gender, too, is produced in marriage, so in legislating in support of marriage, federal and state lawmakers sought to protect a gender order that they believed had been threatened by the war. Lawmakers had first identified the threat in the images and words men shared in U.S. Army camps during the war. After the war, and increasingly sustained by popular support, the state moved to criminalize several types of sexual expression and to regulate the most intimate of human relations.

The New York YMCA had not sought an alliance with doctors on this issue, having defined pornography and its effects, mental and physical, on young men as their chief concern. The convergence of their efforts was nonetheless fortuitous. The YMCA worked for two years to get legislators to pass the New York antipornography law when doctors lent their support to the effort in return for adding the abortion and birth control wording or, as the YMCA recorded it, "some evils untouched."[27] Pornography had been among the YMCA's earliest concerns when in 1863 Frank Ballard addressed members of the YMCA about the evils of "licentious literature," about which he provided few details except that these books were "sold along our streets, at our wharves, and in some of our book-stores." He could provide no sense of the scope of the problem but was sure that the "statistics of this prolific source of sin and suffering ... would startle and sicken us all."[28] From New York, the YMCA expanded their efforts to the U.S. Army camp, where their agents in the U.S. Christian Commission (USCC) distributed bibles, religious tracts, and other books through a loan library system.[29] USCC executives directed a protest to congressmen against "selling secular Reading matter in the Army"—here, "secular" served as an umbrella term for all sorts of reading that the USCC found objectionable, including the "yellow-covered literature" that most troubled them.[30] A few days after the USCC registered its concerns, Congress outlawed the mailing of obscene materials through the U.S. Mail. The YMCA cheered the effort, but by the following year they were at work on the state law that outlawed the sale, distribution, and possession of a long list of items—including those added by their physician allies—and that enlisted the city's policemen in its enforcement. As a result of the YMCA's efforts, the 1868 New York ban on porn was strengthened in 1869 and again in 1872.[31] Within a few years, Maryland's and New York's efforts were replicated in other states, where legislatures passed prohibitions and strengthened them, convincing YMCA antipornography advocates that the time was right to propose a stronger federal measure.

In 1872, the YMCA's new Committee for the Suppression of Vice determined to follow up the successful legislation in New York with a federal law. Late in his enlistment with the Seventeenth Connecticut, Anthony Comstock was drawn to the USCC. After the war, Comstock enlisted with the YMCA and its antipornography project; by the fall of 1871 he began investigating and informing on dealers in New York. Comstock registered his first citizen's arrest in March 1872, followed by fourteen more in the next eight months. Early the next year, in response to a request by the YMCA's Committee for the Suppression of Vice, Comstock prepared a report summarizing his first year of antipornography work, describing what had been a heroic effort on his part:

Obscene photographs, stereoscopic and other pictures, more than 182,000; obscene books and pamphlets, more than 5 tons; obscene letter-press in sheets, more than 2 tons; sheets of impure songs, catalogues, handbills, & c., more than 21,000; obscene microscopic watch and knife charms and graphs and stereoscopic views, about 625; obscene engraved steel and copper plates, 350; obscene lithographic stones destroyed, 20; obscene wood-cut engravings, more than 500; stereographic plates for printing obscene books, more than 5 tons; obscene transparent playing cards, 5,500 to 6,000; obscene and immoral rubber articles, over 30,000; lead moulds for manufacturing rubber goods, twelve sets, or more than 700 pounds; newspapers seized, about 4,600; letters from all parts of the country, ordering these goods, about 15,000; names of dealers in account books seized, about 6,000; list of names in the hands of dealers, that are sold as merchandise, to forward catalogues and circulars to, independent of letters and account books, seized, more than 7,000; arrest of dealers since October 9, 1871, over 50.

Here were the "statistics of this prolific source of sin and suffering" that Frank Ballard had been at pains to provide a decade before. And the numbers were impressive—perhaps too much so. Comstock found a war he could fight, and he had already begun to tally the casualties, adding, ominously, at the end of his report, "publishers, manufacturers and dealers dead since March last, 6."[32] Although Comstock had killed no one—he fancied that the men had died of fear while awaiting trial—the failed soldier found redemption in beginning his own body count.[33] Among the dead was George Ackerman, publisher of *Venus Miscellany*, pioneer in the business of selling erotica through the mail. Comstock trailed and cornered Ackerman in a hotel, forcing the publisher to turn over his stock of books and French playing cards. Ackerman died soon after his arrest.[34]

New York congressman Clinton L. Merriam addressed members

of the Forty-Second U.S. Congress on March 1, 1873, the last day of the session, carrying with him Anthony Comstock's report in support of S. No. 1572, "An Act for the Suppression of Trade in, and Circulation of Obscene Literature and Articles of Immoral Use." He opened with strong words in support of a federal antipornography measure before the House, beseeching congressmen to act on behalf "of the outraged manhood of our age" to ban the trade "which threatens to destroy the future of this Republic by making merchandise of the morals of our youth. Recent revelations have convinced us that no home, how carefully guarded, no school however select, has been safe from these corrupting influences." No "war, pestilence, or famine could leave deeper or more deadly scars upon a nation than the general diffusion of this pestilential literature," Merriam continued; the future of the republic depended on congressmen to rescue "the vigor and purity of our youth."[35] Merriam's comparison of pornography to war in its threat to "our youth" and the nation's future caught the essence of that first measure, passed during the Civil War; with the outcome of the war uncertain, congressmen had sought to save the vigor of the fighting men and, they hoped, to win the war.[36] Now, though, lawmakers feared that the threat went beyond the men, reaching into the most intimate spaces of life, schools and homes. To underscore the point, Merriam added, "The purity and beauty of womanhood have been no protection from the insults of the trade." Nowhere in Merriam's speech did he mention abortion or birth control, but as had been the case in the antipornography laws passed at the state level, items associated with both were now routinely added to long lists of prohibited objects—obscene daguerreotypes, for instance, or stereoscopic pictures, transparent playing cards, or "obscene microscopic watch[es] and knife charms." The rich language of "outraged manhood" spoke to the spirit of the moment; men facing a threat to marriage, to family, should be moved to act to protect their homes, where the "purity and beauty of womanhood" had been unable to. It helped, too, that Comstock had been in Washington since December displaying various items that he had confiscated to members of Congress. Congressmen responded, passing the law with no debate.[37] Although Merriam encouraged lawmakers to "incite every State Legislature to enact similar laws," he needn't have.

In enacting the federal antiobscenity act, or Comstock Law, as it would be called, after the man charged with enforcing it, congressmen rode a rising tide of interest in such laws, and many hailed from states that had similar statutes on the books. The measure was in step with the reform urges of the era for, as historian Susan Pearson has argued, moral reformers were convinced that "the Civil War had been a grand demonstration of the power of coercive government action to purge the nation of sin."[38] The powerful Woman's Christian Temperance Union, founded the same year that the federal measure was passed, endorsed the measure, and union members were willing informants.[39] Anthony Comstock was alone and alienated in the U.S. Army during the war, but his postwar career against pornography and other attendant obscenities aligned well with popular opinion sanctioning the moral authority of the state. The proliferation of state measures indicates broad consensus.

A legacy of the Civil War, pornography was now widely available, in a growing number of forms distributed by a variety of means. Of the items listed in Comstock's report, many had been developed during the war years. The erotic images reproduced by woodcuts or steel and copper plates were large and easy to identify; in their arrests on Nassau Street in the 1850s New York City policemen confiscated and destroyed plates such as these. The more than six hundred "obscene microscopic watch and knife charms" Comstock identified likely referred to Stanhope microphotographs—called "peeps" because of their erotic subject matter. Invented by René Dagron in 1859, these bead-sized images, equipped with a magnifying surface, were mounted in rings, heads of walking sticks, opera glasses, and pistol handles, for instance, allowing viewers to enjoy them discretely in public (fig. 19).[40] Even the most vigilant observers might overlook a well-placed peep.

Before the state Comstock laws, police officers had often been

Fig. 19. Developed in France in 1859, Stanhopes were miniaturized photographs embedded in glass lenses that were installed in everyday objects and could be enjoyed discretely. The Kinsey Institute owns a large selection of Stanhopes. Shown here is a collection and one as it would have looked when viewed. (Photo: sol Legault; courtesy Kinsey Institute)

uninterested or even obstructionist in responding to "informers" or "citizens" making arrests, but now they too were put on notice.[41] Dealers in erotica, particularly those within reach of New York City and Special Agent to the U.S. Post Office Anthony Comstock, used the mail—or advertised in newspapers, circulated pamphlets, or displayed their wares on the street—at their own peril. Comstock kept a close tally of his victories over these "vile dealers in obscenity," similar to how he had kept track in his wartime diary of his defeats over self-impulse. And the body count grew: by end of his career Comstock counted not by numbers but railroad cars full of people and pornography.[42] He was responsible for the spectacular arrest of Madame Restell, a prominent New York abortionist, and others less well known, but Comstock counted fewer overall victories against medical providers, as few physicians proved willing to test the ban on

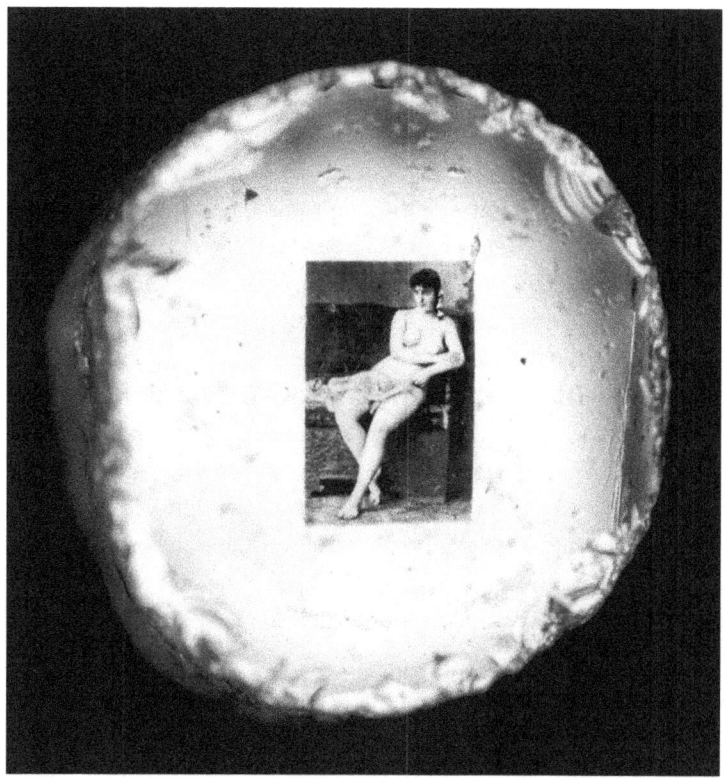

birth control and abortion. Restell committed suicide while awaiting trial in 1878, as did several other men and women arrested by Comstock for providing medical advice or dispensing drugs to women.[43]

Comstock had always had a singular imagination, in which the "young person" imperiled was a man and his sexual imagination. He had been alerted to the problem as a young recruit at war, surrounded by men, a male culture, and feelings that confused him. Comstock recorded in his diary his alienation and his frustration with men who did not share his feelings. He now stood behind a powerful federal measure that would allow him to change men, or at least that is what he imagined. President Ulysses Grant signed the Comstock Law, along with more than two hundred other laws, on

March 3, 1873, the last day of the second session of the Forty-Second Congress. In his report that Clinton Merriam read before Congress, Comstock celebrated the president's refusal to pardon a number of arrested publishers who had appealed to him for clemency.[44] But Grant would prove to be a fickle friend, pardoning two men arrested by Comstock just eight months after signing his name to the law,[45] and then the president betrayed Comstock again in January 1874, when he pardoned two men convicted of "mailing obscene books & c."[46] In his diary, Comstock poured out his frustration, condemning the president's "ignorance" and moaning, "O, that I had known of this in time to have got the facts before Grant. It would not have been granted."[47] It is tempting to read Grant's lukewarm support of antipornography as reflecting his years spent as a soldier, surrounded by a sexual culture that discomfited Comstock. But Grant's pardons may have been motivated by concerns over Special Agent Anthony Comstock's methods, which included deception and entrapment.[48] Such clemency, in any case, captured the spirit of Grant's presidency, for in 1872 the Forty-Second Congress had passed and Grant signed the Amnesty Act removing voting and office-holding restrictions on nearly all-remaining former Confederates, an important step in ending Reconstruction.[49] President Rutherford B. Hayes also disappointed Comstock when he pardoned Ezra Heywood for circulating a free love pamphlet that attacked traditional marriage; in reviewing the case, Hayes determined that the pamphlet was not obscene.[50]

Of course, only a handful of those arrested were pardoned. And the laws passed in the closing days of the Civil War, and in the months and years afterward, by congressmen concerned about protecting marriage and domestic relations remained on the books. An attempt to protect soldiers from their erotic imaginations, leaving them unmanned and incapacitated, left an enduring legal legacy. Laws against pornography and those outlawing abortion and contraception lingered well into the twentieth century. Anthony Comstock, who had been the subject of army pranks, became the butt of jokes, like the image in figure 20. Critics coined the term "Comstockery" to de-

The Postwar Antipornography Campaign 99

"Your Honor, this woman gave birth to a naked child!"

Fig. 20. Illustrations lampooning Anthony Comstock as a prude became common stock by the early twentieth century, like this one by Robert Minor, but they obscure the origins of popular antipornography in the reaction to the dramatic events of the U.S. Civil War. (*The Masses*, 6, no. 12 [September 1915]: 19; courtesy Van Pelt Library, University of Pennsylvania)

scribe overzealous censorship in the name of protecting "the morals of the young," an expression comparable to Dickens's "podsnappery," although the latter seemed to enjoy a shorter shelf life.[51] Comstock, who fancied himself an heir to a great line of British reformers, those behind the 1857 Campbell Act, for instance, embraced the term when he defined it as the "applying of the noblest principles of law, as defined by the Higher Courts of Great Britain and the United States of America, in the interest of Public Morals, especially those of the young.'"[52] Congressman Merriam goaded members of the Forty-Second U.S. Congress to endorse the federal antipornography law when he reminded them that "English men deal less tenderly than we in what tends to demoralize their youth." And so they did, perhaps in part to keep up with the British or perhaps because the stuff was everywhere and to speak against the measure was tantamount to an endorsement.

American pornography was nurtured in the context of transatlantic control and prosecution. "We are told that the number of such books sold annually in New York amounts to 100,000," noted Henry Spencer Ashbee approvingly in his survey. But, like Europe, "America has also its Mr. Collette in a Mr. A. J. Comstock, who 'has succeeded, in the course of a few years, in confiscating and destroying over thirteen tons of this class of publications.'"[53] Comstock would have approved of the comparison to Charles Hastings Collette, secretary of Great Britain's Society for the Suppression of Vice, as Collette was responsible for raiding the London studio of an artist who produced sculptures of nudes. Before Comstock, American antipornography efforts took cues from court decisions and legislative efforts in Europe. After Comstock the reverse was at times true; for example, in 1884 the British Parliament banned pornography from the mail and prohibited its advertisement in 1889, following American precedent.[54] It is fitting that the federal government eventually helped to underwrite the unraveling of this Civil War legacy and did so in the same transatlantic push and pull. The British government only slowly shook off the lingering effects of the antivice campaign to distribute condoms to soldiers during World War I, despite a staggering problem with venereal disease. The American government moved even slower, following suit only in World War II.

The U.S. Civil War bisected two periods of antipornography activism and determined activists' particular focus on men as its victims. The war came at a time when consensus about what constituted the obscene was breaking down and yet, because of new printing technologies, obscene words and images seemed to be everywhere. Many of these were headed to the soldiers fighting in the war. The Union

Army brought together men with different understandings about what defined one as a man and how to go about achieving manhood. At times, obscene words and images helped to smooth over these differences, becoming part of the sexual culture of the camp where men like Second Lieutenant James Graham enjoyed and shared them and kept on soldiering and men like Colonel Ebenezer Peirce nearly lost his command. Pornography shared between soldiers served as a disciplinary regime that might sustain the prerogatives of rank or subvert them. Sharing obscene words and images—looks and touches, even—was an affirmation of life amidst death. Civilian lawmakers operating outside this cultural milieu sought to restrain it, because the nation was at risk and because, they suspected, so was marriage.

To sustain marriage, after the war state and national lawmakers passed measures aimed at controlling a broad range of items deemed obscene, not by a common definition of the term but, rather, by lists of items that just kept getting longer with each new, stricter measure. On these lists were a growing number of pornographic media, attesting to the persistence of demand and a desire to fill it and to a growing popular consensus that obscenity ought to be criminalized. To the lists of banned items were added contraceptive devices, abortifacients, and a variety of services intended to help women avoid pregnancy. The lists here, too, got longer, but fewer doctors were willing to test the ban than there were pornographers—and the risks to the consumers of banned items were never comparable.

Over time, we became less concerned with protecting the "young person" from porn, yet even when the consensus shifted, we continued to defer to lawmakers who convinced us that marriage ought to be protected from such obscenities—"evils untouched"—as birth control and abortion. That we continue to talk about such things with a faint sense of shame should remind us that, although their origins are intertwined, American antipornography diverged decidedly from Europe's. Whereas in Europe postwar pronatalist policies were sponsored as a response to war's violence—indeed, British law defined abortion as a violence done *to* women—European reformers did not link abortion and birth control to pornography. Since the late twentieth century, such questions have been off the table in Europe, with laws liberalizing access to and liberally funding birth control and abortion services. In the United States, postwar reformers who saw in pornography the threat of male violence sponsored measures that committed the state to a policy of pronatalism while relinquishing responsibility to protect "young people" and others from porn and violence. To understand how this came to be, we need to pay attention to the particular circumstances of the U.S. Civil War, the war's violence, and the men who legislated in its aftermath.

It is a supreme irony that the elite men who founded the YMCA in an effort to save young men from the temptations of the city and the U.S. Army camp built an institution that became central to urban gay male identity in the war's aftermath. At the YMCA, men gathered to read, use the gymnasium, and swim; they rented rooms, too, as the Y promised to provide young men a temporary and safe alternative to family life. By the turn of the century, though, as historian George Chauncey has shown, Y's had become meccas both for young men who identified as "fairies" and "queers" and for others who did not but who nonetheless sought male sexual company. As in antipornography, police in New York and other cities showed little interest in making arrests in these cases, although they had at their disposal antisodomy laws and other measures to do so. Anthony Comstock first turned the attention of the YMCA's Society for the Suppression of Vice to the threat of sodomy, adding the performances and publications of New York's gay community to the long list of obscenities he was authorized to combat. He organized police raids on clubs and shops that sold gay literature and initiated prosecutions against "moral perverts" and "sodomers"; by 1900 Comstock boasted of having dealt "with a great many [people] of this character," adding his expertise on such matters to his reform resume.[55] Like pornography, homosexuality proved resistant to Comstock's interventions, but combatting it nonetheless became part of a predictable pattern in which reformers enlisted the support of a morally invigorated state in a campaign of postwar sexual regulation. Scholars have not yet uncovered this history, but as is the case with pornography, understanding the sexual culture of the U.S. Army camp will likely bring us closer to doing so.

EPILOGUE

During the Civil War, men who had seen and participated in extraordinary acts of violence had also at times enjoyed unprecedented access to sexually explicit publications. Neither the violence nor the porn was consistent with the middle-class values of restraint or respectability. Lawmakers sought to outlaw the pornography because they worried that the Union might lose the war. Others, including Anthony Comstock, worried about not how porn might impact the war but what it did to young men. Few asked what the *violence* might do to men, but among them was Calvin Blanchard, "a free love iconoclast" who condemned the hypocrisy of a government that sent men to die even as it sought to protect their morals.[1] The most obscene thing in life, Blanchard wrote in his 1864 book, *Art of Real Pleasure*, was war. In the book, a time traveler finds himself in wartime New York City where he buys a newspaper and is shocked to learn of the Civil War. He reads of "the bones of Yankees, that bleach on the plains of Northern Virginia, if piled in a row, would make a macadamized road from Richmond to Washington." And there is more: "Twenty thousand Unionists burnt alive or torn to pieces by blood hounds! Fifty thousand secesh and forty thousand loyalists killed in the great battle! No quarter on either side! Two million women and children starving to death in Dixie! Richmond taken! Six thousand prisoners blown sky high! The rioters burning New York and trying to murder all black men, women, and children, together with those who would protect them." The traveler "drops the paper in horror."[2]

Art of Real Pleasure sold like most other erotic literature, through widely circulated catalogs advertising cheap, small books, perhaps with yellow covers, mailed discretely to buyers. "The ART OF REAL PLEASURE," Blanchard promised in one such advertisement, "is the most sensuous book ever written. It's the great secret revealed, of perfect gratification, without troublesome consequences. It's just what every man and every woman wants." The book opens with a sexual encounter between the narrator and a "nymph" with "hazle-brown eyes. Her ringlets fell over a neck and shoulders of matchless form and symmetry. Her breasts were of a charmingness surpassing all description . . . she was absolute perfection."[3] The reader is then told, following the commitment- and consequence-free sexual encounter, the secret to a society based on free love principles.

There is not much left of Civil War–era erotica, tucked away as it is in private collections and not generally collected by academic institutions. *Art of Real Pleasure* was reprinted in the 1970s, perhaps because its political message spoke to a countercultural "make love not war" moment. Written during the Civil War as a critique of that generation's war and a moral reform campaign that ignored it, the book spoke to the young disillusioned with Vietnam. Thomas Lowry's collection of Civil War pornography was published in 1994, around the time that Americans' fascination with the Civil War began to grow. By then Operation Desert Storm, touted as a "bloodless war" (for Americans), made war fashionable again, and the Internet, of course, was making porn more accessible. Americans do not generally think of our love of war, and particularly the Civil War, as pornographic, but as Drew Gilpin Faust has suggested, in our obsessive fascination with the war we are "not so different from those New Yorkers who in 1862 crowded in to see Mathew Brady's photographs of the Antietam dead."[4] And she makes a good point, for whereas porn retains, in the post-Comstock era, the aura of a failure of personal restraint and the need to be secret, looking at war, in pictures or print, is respectable.

Writing about war remains respectable, too. Faust asks, "In writing about war, even against war, do we nevertheless reinforce its attraction and affirm its meaning?"[5] We might properly ask, too, which of us who writes about the Civil War is not also at times reproducing war's obscenity? In his classic study *The Other Victorians*, Steven Marcus coined the term "pornotopia" to describe not only the literary genre of pornography but also what is produced when an author attempts to sum up, sort out, and synthesize such works.[6] Like utopias, pornography exists outside of time and place; it produces a familiar geography that Marcus describes as follows: "It is represented at eye level. In the middle distance there looms a large irregular shape. On the horizon swell two immense snowy white hillocks. . . . The landscape then undulates gently down to a broad, smooth, swelling plain, its soft rolling curves broken only in the lower center."[7] And pornography is not so much about human beings as it is about "juxtapositions of human bodies, parts of bodies, limbs, and organs; they are depictions of positions and events, diagrammatic schema for sexual ballets—actually they are more like football plays than dances; they are at any rate as complicated as either."[8] Quoting a scene from the anonymous 1873 novel *The Romance of Lust*, Marcus makes his point: "So to five women we thus add six men, and eventually a very handsome young priest, debauched by the others, joined our party, and we carried on the wildest and most extravagant orgies of every excess the most raging lust could devise." Then the following pages work out the mathematical equation of possible couplings, double couplings, and so forth, until all combinations have been tried and repeated; the story then ends, nowhere.[9] "The ideal pornographic novel," Marcus explains, "would go on forever; it would have no ending, just as in pornotopia there is no such thing as time."[10]

Are there parallels between writing porn and writing about the Civil War? To test out Marcus's notion of pornotopia, in particular the geography and arithmetic it produces, we might turn to a book published in 2013 to coincide with the 150th anniversary of the Battle of Gettysburg. In the opening pages we are treated to an eye-level description of south-central Pennsylvania as a wide "plain, full of pleats and tucks" that "subsides into a series of low-lying ridges that parallel South Mountain itself as if they were undulations from the mountain's upthrust, until one by one they gradually expend their height and their force sixty miles away at the Susquehanna."[11] An anthropomorphized Cemetery Ridge snakes "southward to a pair of desolate, upthrust granite hills."[12] Not all hills are desolate, of course, as Culp's Hill is "thickly wooded eminence," and some are better than others—Cemetery Hill, of course, with its particular elevation and its thick "spine" made "'an artilleryman grow enthusiastic.'"[13] Even a familiar geography can sound mysterious when described from eye level: Gettysburg's upthrust or undulating hills might be Pennsylvania, Virginia, or even the little province of Walloon Brabant, Belgium, south of Waterloo.

While Gettysburg shares the geography of pornotopia, the makeshift hospitals reproduce its anonymous arithmetic. Shells blow apart bodies, shots mangle limbs, and "rifle bullets smash and splatter." And then there are the amputations that come fast and furious until, like Carl Schurz, we are "unnerved" by the "'arms and legs in heaps' sometimes 'more than man high.'" "One 3rd Corps surgeon 'performed at the least calculation fifty amputations,'" fourteen of them at one stretch "'without leaving the table.'"[14] In the book's final chapter, the author calculates the battle's gruesome arithmetic, equating the Confederates' losses of nearly twenty thousand to "two sinkings of the Titanic, the 2001 attacks on the World Trade Center and the Pentagon, ten repetitions of the Great Blizzard of 1888, and two Pearl Harbors."[15] For readers who find that math too obscure, historian Allen Guelzo offers another equation: at Gettysburg, the Army of Northern Virginia alone "sustained two and half times the losses taken by the Allied armies in Normandy from D-Day through August 1944."[16] Having played out the arithmetic, the story comes to an end—until the next one comes along offering a new arithmetic played out on a familiar geography. Allen Guelzo's 2013 book, *Gettysburg: The Last Invasion*, is a fine book that critics agreed provided a fresh and gritty portrait of the three-day battle; it was awarded the prestigious Gilder Lehrman Lincoln Prize, among other awards.[17] In its intimate and graphic discussion of the battle and the field on which it was fought, books like this reproduce the mathematics and the logic of Steven Marcus's pornotopia.

Blanchard wrote *Art of Real Pleasure* to condemn the hypocrisy of a nation that sought to solve one obscenity—slavery—by perpetrating another: war. Readers might detect a similar hypocrisy in a book about the Civil War that offers an implicit criticism of books about the Civil War. About Blanchard we know very little except that he produced a number of books with a similar social message.[18] About me, as I have said, I came to this topic through my training in gender and the Civil War; my work has focused on women's experiences of war and the consequences of the war to soldier families and others on the home front. When I was in graduate school, pornography and whether and how the government should control it were divisive topics; they continue to be. A modern feminist critique of pornography holds that it encourages men to be violent, a claim not unlike Comstock's, except that feminists are concerned about women as the victims of violence. Comstock never provided any evidence of the link between obscene words and images and violence, and indeed, modern feminist claims about the connections between pornography and rape remain unproven. In tackling this subject, I have been struck by how violence existed alongside of erotic images and words, with neither eliciting a groundswell of concern until the Civil War's epic violence came to an end. Today, pornography is much more violent and much more available then in the mid-nineteenth century—it really is "here and there and everywhere"—and yet we evidence little ambition to control it. We remain concerned that its worst effects are felt among "youth," but instead of investing the state with authority to intervene, we rely on parental vigilance. Paying attention to the ways in which our writing about war at times reproduces some of what concerns us about pornography is, it seems to me, another kind of vigilance, one that we owe our readers, "young people" and others.

NOTES

Introduction

1. Section 3, for instance, protected "loyal postmasters" if they were robbed by Confederates or their offices destroyed, section 11 prohibited delivery of suspicious mail to foreign addresses, and section 14 provided for fines and other punishments for those who destroyed offices or injured postmasters. "Postal Laws," *Congressional Globe*, 38th Cong., 2nd sess., no. 61, Feb. 21, 1865, 965–66. The bill was proposed and debated on Feb. 8, and the vote was called on Feb. 21.

2. "Postal Laws," *Congressional Globe*, 38th Cong., 2nd sess., no. 42, Feb. 8, 1865, 660–61.

3. Collamer admitted that he was "not perhaps entirely satisfied" with the section allowing postmasters to identify and destroy mail. Ibid., 660–61.

4. One senator worried that pornography might even corrupt postmasters charged with handling it. For that reason, he insisted Congress not give them power to seize suspect mail. "After the postmaster takes the material out, what is he to do with it? May he circulate it as he thinks proper?" Maryland's Reverdy Johnson asked. Congressmen discussed how these materials were usually sent, unsealed or open at one end and all insisted that postmasters would be able to identify obscene materials easily. Ibid., 661.

5. Ibid.

6. Register of Arrests for Offenses against the Postal Laws, 1:46.

7. "Obituary: Benjamin H. Day," *New York Herald*, Dec. 22, 1889, 20; Dennis, *Licentious Gotham*, 48.

8. J. S. Colgate, arrested June 2, 1870, in New York City for "mailing obscene books &c, &c., &c," was found guilty in U.S. circuit court and sentenced to a year in prison and a $5,000 fine. Register of Arrests for Offenses against the Postal Laws, 2:45.

9. Quoted in Broun and Leech, *Roundsman of the Lord*, 14–15.

10. Mohr, *Abortion in America*, 97.

11. Brainerd, *Christian Work*, 5–18.

12. J. W. Waldron, Chaplain 31st N.Y. Regiment, to Rev. Stephen Tyng Jr., N.Y., July 3, 1863; and Charles A. Beck, 26th Penn. Regiment, Washington, D.C., to Tyng, July 10, 1861, both in Kautz Family YMCA Archives, box 336.

13. U.S. Sanitary Commission for the Army and Navy, Third Annual Report, Philadelphia, Pa., 1865, 47–51, Kautz Family YMCA Archives, box 2.

14. *Miller v. California*, 413 U.S. 15 (1973), quoted in Legal Information Institute, "Obscenity."

One way to measure the distance between today's "community standards" and those of the Civil War and postwar generation would be to consider how attendees at a 2012 conference where this work was first presented referred to the project as "Fifty Shades of Blue and Gray," a reference to the 2011 erotic romance novel *Fifty Shades of Grey* by E. L. James that was widely read and that, according to one source, became the "fastest selling paperback of all time" (Paul Bentley, "'Mummy Porn'"). The comparison was intended as a wry commentary on Victorian sexual prudery as well as a reference to the moneymaking potential of writing a book about porn and the Civil War.

15. Historian Helen Lefkowitz Horowitz identifies federal censorship of mail as part of what she calls the first culture war, in which a variety of Americans engaged in "sexual conversation" (*Rereading Sex*, 299).

16. Whites, "Civil War as a Crisis in Gender," 10.

17. Silber, *Romance of Reunion*, 19.

18. Foote, *Gentlemen and the Roughs*; Greenberg, *Manifest Manhood*.

19. For prostitution, see Clinton, "'Public Women,'" 61–77. Rape, too, has recently been the subject of scholarly interest; see Barber and Ritter, "'Physical Abuse.'"

20. Jeffords, *Remasculinization of America*, xv.

21. Lowry, *Story the Soldiers Wouldn't Tell*, 1.22. The publisher did not share sales data, but in correspondence Lowry revealed that the book has sold an enviable 32,000 copies in the twenty-one years it had been out. Thomas P. Lowry, e-mail message to author, Aug. 7, 2015.

23. Faust, "'We Should Grow Too Fond of It,'" 368–83.

24. Reviews of Lowry, *Story the Soldiers Wouldn't Tell*, at Amazon, http://www.amazon.com/The-Story-Soldiers-Wouldnt-Tell/product-reviews/0811711536/ref=cm_cr_dp_see_all_btm?ie=UTF8&showViewpoints=1&sortBy=bySubmissionDateDescending (accessed May 3, 2013).

25. Higonnet, Jenson, Michel, and Weitz, *Behind the Lines*, 3–4.

26. When the men in Company G, Ninety-Fifth Illinois Regiment, found out years later that Albert Cashier was actually Jennie Hodgers, they continued referring to Jennie as "he." "We sometimes called him half and half," said Robert Horan, one of Hodgers's comrades, recalling her time as a soldier. Quoted in Leonard, *All the Daring*, 186.

27. Massey, "Effects of Shortages," 188–89. Kurt O. Berends in "'Wholesome Reading'" found church-sponsored religious newspapers working hard through-

out the war to win over the hearts of Confederate soldiers with a message of moral uplift. Surely there is more to the story. Despite antiliteracy laws, the Old South was full of readers, Beth Barton Schweiger argues in "Literate South," supplied via a growing number of post offices, bookstores, Sunday schools, libraries, academies, and college libraries ("The Literate South," 335–36).

Chapter 1

1. Kendrick, *Secret Museum*, 129.
2. Pisanus Fraxi, *Index Librorum*, xxxi.
3. Kendrick, *Secret Museum*, 115–17.
4. Ibid., 117.
5. *Oxford English Dictionary Online*, s.v. "pornography," http://www.oed.com (accessed June 1, 2012).
6. Hunt, *Invention of Pornography*, 15.
7. Kendrick, *Secret Museum*, 125.
8. Karen Halttunen argues that humanitarian "reformers were caught up in the same cultural linkages of revulsion with desire that fueled a wide range of popular literary explorations of pain" ("Humanitarianism and the Pornography of Pain," 29).
9. *The People (A. Oakey Hall, District Attorney) v. Thomas Ormsby and John Atchison*, Feb. 23, 1855, New York District Attorney's Indictment Papers.
10. Sworn statement of James Twain [sic?], ibid., Feb. 15, 1855.
11. Dennis, *Licentious Gotham*, 4.
12. Fernando Wood to A. Oakley Hall, *People v. Ormsby and Atchison*, Feb. 28, 1855.
13. *The People (A. Oakey Hall, District Attorney) v. Terence Morris*, *The People (A. Oakey Hall, District Attorney) v. Arthur Crown*, and *The People (A. Oakey Hall, District Attorney) v. John Farrell*, Mar. 12, 1855, New York District Attorney's Indictment Papers.
14. The original 1842 ban on obscene imports mentioned only "prints" and "pictures," whereas the 1857 revision added daguerreotypes, photographs, images, figures, and "all other 'obscene articles.'" Paul and Schwartz, *Federal Censorship*, 17.
15. Dennis, *Licentious Gotham*, 3.
16. Hawley, "American Publishers," 347.
17. Ibid., 359–63.
18. Ibid., 496–503.
19. Yellow paper was machine produced using straw fibers and dyed yellow. "Yellow-covered" books flourished in the antebellum period, but not all were erotica. The American Tract Society's *Family Christian Almanac* was also in cheap yellow binding, as were city guides, almanacs, rail guides, theater playbills, and minstrel songbooks. Ibid., 166.
20. Ibid., 133.
21. Ibid., 323–31, 346–48.

22. Dennis, *Licentious Gotham*, 170–82.

23. Hawley, "American Publishers," 275–76.

24. Ibid., 421. Historian Helen Lefkowitz Horowitz notes that because sexually explicit materials were often destroyed to avoid prosecution, they were never catalogued by the Library of Congress (*Rereading Sex*, 217).

25. Thomas Ormsby, "Thomas Ormsby's Commission Bureau and General Purchasing Agency," 1861, American Broadsides and Ephemera, American Antiquarian Society.

26. "Genuine Fancy Books: Beautifully Illustrated with Colored Plates," 186–, American Broadsides and Ephemera, American Antiquarian Society.

27. Hawley, "American Publishers," 284.

28. "Postmasters," *Venus Miscellany*, Jan. 31, 1857, quoted in Dennis, *Licentious Gotham*, 185–86n55.

29. "Great Seizures of Obscene Literature," *New York Herald*, Sept. 16, 1857, 8.

30. Dennis, *Licentious Gotham*, 190–98.

31. According to the Smithsonian National Postal Museum, by 1862 mail was sorted en route, as a train moved between two points. http://postalmuseum.si.edu/RMS/history/mailbyrail.html (accessed March 23, 2016).

32. Horowitz, *Rereading Sex*, 310–12.

33. W. H., "Morals of Our Soldiers," *Christian Recorder*, Aug. 31, 1861.

34. Patrick, *Inside Lincoln's Army*, 255–56, entry dated June 8, 1863.

35. "From Washington," *Philadelphia Inquirer*, June 15, 1863, 1.

36. "Army 'Leeches'—New York 'Fancy Men' in Camp—Present Appearance of Fredericksburg—Condition of the Army, &c." *New York Daily Tribune*, Aug. 23, 1862, 2.

37. M. G. Tousley, Capt., Blue Springs, Tenn., to Abraham Lincoln, Mar. 23, 1864, quoted in Michael Musick, "Spirited and Spicy Scenes?," 12. The original letter is supposed to be located at the National Archives, RG 107, Letters Received, Secretary of War, no. T-291 (130), but I was unable to locate it in the microfilmed records of the Secretary of War.

38. Baker, *History of the United States Secret Service*, 382–83.

39. Hunt, *Invention of Pornography*, 12.

40. Kendrick, *Secret Museum*, 31, 118.

41. Halttunen, "Humanitarianism and the Pornography of Pain," 324.

42. Testimony of Monsieur C. C. Robin, quoted in Weld, *American Slavery*, 59.

43. Walters, "Erotic South," 183.

44. Stowe, *Uncle Tom's Cabin*, 440. Teresa A. Goddu places Harriet Beecher Stowe's work in the tradition of American gothic literature and analyzes how, in Stowe's hands, "the event of slavery is structured in gothic terms" (*Gothic America*, 143). Instead of confronting the worst of slavery head on, Stowe employed such evasive gothic conventions as ghosts, for example, when Legree's house is haunted by the screams of a slave who was imprisoned and beaten to death in an attic garret (*Uncle Tom's Cabin*, 425).

45. Stowe, *Uncle Tom's Cabin*, 352.
46. "Uncle Tom's Cabin," *National Era*, Apr. 15, 1852, 63.
47. Thompson, *City Crimes*, 190. Thompson went by several pen names, including Greenhorn, Green Horn, and Paul de Kock. *City Crimes* was published "by Greenhorn."
48. Garrison, "Address to the Colonization Society."
49. "Saul and Webster," *Liberator*, Mar. 18, 1853, 43. Nonslaveholding Southerners used the term as well. See Helper, *Impending Crisis*, 121.
50. Clay, "Amalgamation Series."
51. Kendrick, *Secret Museum*, 123.
52. These estimates are based on average birth year of soldiers in the Army of the Potomac and the Army of Northern Virginia. Joseph Glatthaar found that the median age of Union soldiers was one year younger than Confederate soldiers. More telling, while three in every five Confederate soldiers had children at home, only one in five Union soldiers was a father. Glatthaar, "Tale of Two Armies."

Chapter 2

1. Court-martial of Col. Ebenezer Peirce, 29th Regiment, Mass. Vols., U.S. Army Courts-Martial, II835, Apr. 1862.
2. Dennis, *Art/Porn*, 12.
3. Although Peirce was found guilty on many of the charges filed against him and the court recommended dismissal, the ruling was overturned by Peirce's superior officer. Bowen, *Massachusetts in the War*, 435–51.
4. Hunt, *Colonels in Blue*, 120.
5. Peirce court-martial, Exhibit A, Ebenezer W. Peirce to Mr. President and the Honorable Court, Apr. 14, 1862, 3.
6. Peirce court-martial, Exhibit B, Ebenezer Peirce written statement, Apr. 18, 1862, 10–11.
7. Ibid., 3–4.
8. Peirce court-martial, 21.
9. Hunt, *Invention of Pornography*, 44.
10. To identify these cases, I searched Thomas Lowry's U.S. Army Courts-Martial search database of 75,964 cases for the following terms, either quoted in the original case or employed as a marker by Lowry: "obscene/obscenity," "profane/profanity," "lewd," "playing cards," and "carte de visite." The terms "pornography" or "porn" came into wide use after the war, and though we added these terms, they yielded no hits. I added the terms "profane" and "profanity," on Lorien Foote's advice, because using profane language was often associated with other sorts of bad behavior, such as trading in obscene images. The searches yielded fifty-seven hits. I eliminated the thirteen courts-martial that named playing cards, because none of them indicated a concern for the circulation of obscene images or words. Of the forty-four that remained, most referred to the "lewd" character of women with whom men kept company, a soldier's "obscene language," or soldiers

who wrote "obscene" letters, such as Private Noah Johnson, Seventh Artillery, New York, who admitted to having written a "filthy and obscene" letter on behalf of Private William Stalker, who was illiterate, to Stalker's mother (court-martial of Private Noah Johnson, 7th N.Y. Artillery, U.S. Army Courts-Martial, LL103, Jan. 1, 1863). The four cases that specifically named obscene images or publications are discussed in this chapter.

11. Dennis, *Licentious Gotham*, 148–49.
12. Ibid., 101–2.
13. Hawley, "American Publishers," 158–59.
14. Peirce court-martial, 22–24.
15. Ibid., James Boothe testimony, 125–29; and Daniel Blaisedell testimony, 129–33.
16. Ibid., 128–29.
17. See Hawley's discussion of the steam-powered Adams power presses that were widely used in 1850s in "American Publishers," 306–11. Manufacturers took advantage of the customs laws and improvements in woodcutting and lithography—the former we usually associate with the lavish battle scenes reproduced in *Harper's Weekly* and the latter with western scenes sold by Currier and Ives—to produce a wide range of cheap erotic images, sometimes created by the same craftsmen. Ibid., 208–41.
18. "Oscanyan's Lecture: A Night in the Harem," *New York Herald*, Dec. 12, 1856, 8.
19. Quoted in Musick, "Spirited and Spicy Scenes?," 27.
20. Cohen, *Murder of Helen Jewett*.
21. Court-martial of 2nd Lieut. William Lyman, 13th New York Heavy Artillery, U.S. Army Courts-Martial, LL1983, April 1, 1864, 12.
22. Ibid., 12–13.
23. Although "beaver shot" is a twentieth-century term, Dennis uses it to explain the sudden appearance of pubic hair, a startling and shocking departure from artistic idealizations of women's bodies. Dennis, *Art/Porn*, 60.
24. Beecher, *Lectures to Young Men*, 124–25.
25. Gallman, "Snapshots: Images of Men," 133–36.
26. S. A. Neel to "Mr. William Neel," Oct. 2, 1864, William Neel Collection, RG 511, 4.
27. Alice Waddell to William Waddell, Camp Curtain, 9th Penn. Calvary, Apr. 26, 1863, Philadelphia Civil War and Underground Railroad Museum Collections. Alice and William had one child, three-year-old Fanny, in 1860, and in her wartime letters to William, Alice mentions a younger daughter named Alle. 1860 Census; Wilkes Barre, Luzerne, Pennsylvania; Roll: M653_1133; Page: 1015; Image: 421; Family History Library Film: 805133, Ancestry.com.
28. Higginson, *Army Life in a Black Regiment*, 82–83.
29. Fussell, *Great War and Modern Memory*, 276.

30. Das, *Touch and Intimacy*, 118. On fraternity, see Yacovone, "'Surpassing the Love of Women,'" 195–215.
31. Barber and Ritter, "Physical Abuse," 51.
32. Galwey, *Valiant Hours*, 71.
33. Ibid., 182, 186.
34. Ibid., 71.
35. Lyman court-martial, testimonies of Lieut. J. C. Hopper, Lieut. Hoffman, and Capt. George Potter, 8, 9, 10–11.
36. Court-martial of Major Lorenzo Phelps, 5th Regiment, (W.) Va. Vol. Infantry, U.S. Army Courts-Martial, MM870, April 1, 1863 12–13.
37. Court-martial of Capt. Hampden Waldron, 5th Regiment, U.S. Veteran Vols., U.S. Army Courts-Martial, MM3915, March 31–May 16, 1866 60, 51–52.
38. Ibid., 53.
39. Ibid.
40. Ibid., Waldron's closing argument, Exhibit Q, 6.
41. Herzog, *Sex after Fascism*, 217.
42. Dennis, *Art/Porn*, 105.
43. Mitchell, *Vacant Chair*, 71–87.
44. Hunt, *Colonels in Blue*, 120.
45. Johnson, *Roaring Camp*, 144.

Chapter 3

1. "The Loss of the 17th Connecticut," *Columbian Register*, July 11, 1863, 2.
2. Noble, "History of the 17th Regiment," 248.
3. Samuel Comstock and Justus Silliman joined the Seventeenth Connecticut in the summer of 1862 and engaged in their first combat at Chancellorsville in May 1863, where the regiment lost more 120 men, at least seven of them from Company H. Ibid., 243; Justus Silliman to "My Dear Mother," May 8–9, 1863, Marcus, *Letters of Justus M. Silliman*, 24–34; Silliman to mother, Sept. 26, 1863, ibid., 48. An image of Samuel's grave is available at http://www.findagrave.com/cgi-bin/fg.cgi?page=pv&GRid=68611160&PIpi=41263129 (accessed March 24, 2016).
4. "1884 Monument Dedication," http://seventeenthcvi.org/blog/gettysburg-excursions/1884-monument-dedication/ (accessed March 11, 2016). Anthony Comstock did join the others at an 1891 reunion in New Canaan. "1891 Reunion at New Canaan," http://seventeenthcvi.org/blog/veterans/1891-reunion/ (accessed March 11, 2016).
5. Trumbull, *Anthony Comstock, Fighter*, 35.
6. Bederman, *Manliness and Civilization*, 18.
7. Foote, *Gentlemen and the Roughs*, 95–97.
8. Trumbull, *Anthony Comstock, Fighter*, 36.
9. Whites, "Crisis in Masculinity."
10. Since late in the twentieth century, the term has also described something

that offends because it is "ridiculously or offensively high," such as prices or profits. *Oxford English Dictionary Online*, s.v. "obscene," http://www.oed.com (accessed June 1, 2012).

11. Hunt, *Invention of Pornography*, 13.

12. See Kendrick's discussion of the 1857 Campbell Act and Chief Justice Cockburn's decision in the 1868 case *Regina v. Hicklin* in *Secret Museum*, 116–23.

13. Chief Justice Cockburn in *Regina v. Hicklin*, quoted in ibid., 121.

14. Dickens, *Our Mutual Friend*, 339. Of course, Dickens's Miss Podsnap is really rather world-wise despite the intense sheltering to which she has been subjected:

> Miss Podsnap's life had been, from her first appearance on this planet, altogether of a shady order; for Mr. Podsnap's young person was likely to get little good out of association with other young persons, and had theretofore been restricted to companionship with not very congenial older persons, and with massive furniture. Miss Podsnap's early views of life being principally derived from the reflections of it in her father's boots. (135)

15. Linderman, *Embattled Courage*, 16. For soldiers' understanding of the relationship between fear and courage, see McPherson, *For Cause and Comrades*, 36–37. See also Foote's discussion of courage and manhood in *Gentlemen and the Roughs*, 57–58.

16. Letter to "Mother," May 31, 1862, in Brewster, *When This Cruel War Is Over*, 141.

17. "No single item was more essential to a respectable household than a collection of books," historian Richard Lyman Bushman explains of the antebellum period, and "no activity more effectual for refinement and personal improvement than reading" (*Refinement of America*, 282).

18. Alcott, *Letters to Young Men*, 85, 76–79; Alcott, *Young Men's Guide*, 203.

19. Erikson, "Welcome to Sodom," 287.

20. Stewart, "Cultural Work," 679.

21. "The Ethics and Humanities of War," *United States Service Magazine*, Feb. 1864, 119, 121.

22. Broun and Leech, *Roundsman of the Lord*, 59.

23. Susan Johnson found a similar experience among men in gold rush California in *Roaring Camp*, 135–44.

24. Silliman to mother, Apr. 19 and 24, 1864, quoted in Graham, "Home Front," 41n79.

25. Ibid., 37–39.

26. Silliman to mother, Apr. 19, 1864, quoted in ibid., 37n68.

27. Ibid., 41.

28. Comstock diary, entry for Jan. 25, 1864, reprinted in Broun and Leech, *Roundsman of the Lord*, 48.

29. Ibid., entry for Mar. 21, 1864, 46.

30. Ibid., entry for Mar. 20, 1864, 46.
31. Ibid., entry for Mar. 4, 1864, 45.
32. Ibid., entry for Mar. 9, 1864, 45.
33. Ibid., entries for April 24, 1864, 53; May 18, 1864, 46; and Dec. 20, 1864, 54.
34. Stott, *Jolly Fellows*, 58–59.
35. One set of early twentieth-century biographers looked in vain for evidence of Comstock's sense of humor, concluding that "his was a soul essentially and profoundly grave." Broun and Leech, *Roundsman of the Lord*, 69–70.
36. Comstock's studying tactics and polishing his gun were reminiscent of "Chickenshit," or what American soldiers in World War II called orders that were "small minded and ignoble" and those that took "the trivial seriously." "Chickenshit can be recognized instantly," Paul Fussell explains, "because it never has anything to do with winning the war" (*Great War and Modern Memory*, 80).
37. Comstock diary, entry for Mar. 9, 1864, reprinted in Broun and Leech, *Roundsman of the Lord*, 45.
38. Trumbull, *Anthony Comstock, Fighter*, 39.
39. Comstock diary, entry for Apr. 24, 1864, reprinted in Broun and Leech, *Roundsman of the Lord*, 53.
40. Ibid., entries for May 18 and 19, 1864, 46.
41. Silliman to mother, Apr. 3, 1864, Marcus, *Letters of Justus M. Silliman*, 67.
42. Ibid., 68.
43. Woodworth, *While God Is Marching On*, 237–39.
44. Comstock diary, entry for May 19, 1864, reprinted in Broun and Leech, *Roundsman of the Lord*, 46.
45. Ibid., entry for July 11, 1864, after p. 46.
46. Ibid., undated entries, 55–56.
47. Ibid., undated entry, 56.
48. Ibid.
49. Trumbull, *Anthony Comstock, Fighter*, 29.
50. Sylvester Graham, *Lecture to Young Men*, 92–93.
51. Fussell, *Great War and Modern Memory*, 272, 273–74.
52. An author of some note before the war, John William De Forest is best known for his 1867 novel *Miss Ravenel's Conversion from Secession to Loyalty*. The editor of his published letters described De Forest before the war as "somewhat dilettantish." James Croushore, introduction to De Forest, *Volunteer's Adventures*, vii.
53. "To come down to a basis," one author insisted, "muscle makes the man." "Misery vs. Muscle," *Frank Leslie's*, February 25, 1860, 192. Another author worried that in a state of peace, "courages effeminate" and manhood softens. "Ethics and Humanities of War," *United States Service Magazine*, February 1864, 119.
54. De Forest, *Volunteer's Adventures*, 230; Hijiya, *J. W. De Forest and the Rise of American Gentility*, 61–62.

55. De Forest, "Sheridan's Battle of Winchester," 199.
56. Jubal Early's army numbered 14,000, and losses were estimated at twenty-five percent. Adelman, "Third Battle of Winchester."
57. De Forest, *Volunteer's Adventures*, 15.
58. Diary of James Graham, Company K, 80th Ohio Infantry Regiment, entries for Mar. 6 and Mar. 16, 1863, Civil War Document Collection, box 48, folder 3.
59. "Finished reading Lewis Ar[. . .]del," ibid., entry for Mar. 29, 1863.
60. Ibid., entry for May 3, 1863.
61. Ibid., entry for May 4, 1863.
62. Anonymous, *Murdered Queen!*
63. Claiming some familiarity with the emotional worlds of young women served Graham well with "the ladies," as he details in later diary entries kissing and "squeezing" a number of young women, as well as carrying on correspondence with many. Graham, "Excerpts from the Diary of a Yankee in Dixie," 32–37.
64. Ibid., 32.
65. McPherson, *Battle Cry*, 626–38.
66. Fryer, *History of the Eightieth Ohio Veteran Volunteer Infantry*, 10.
67. References to regimental order books in this section were identified using Lorien Foote's survey of the surviving regimental order books of twenty-six regiments. Foote, *Gentlemen and the Roughs*, 182.
68. C. E. Griswold & Col. Comdy, 56th Mass. Regimental Order Book, General Order 29, Feb. 14, 1864, Camp Meigs, Readville, Mass.
69. First Lieut. Henry Allen and Acting Adjutant General James Hubbell, Mar. 20, 1864, Book Records of Volunteer Union Organizations, 17th Conn. Regimental Order Book, Companies G to K.
70. First Lieut. Col. A. H. Wilcoxson and George Peck Acting Adjutant, May 27, 1864, General Order 99, ibid.
71. First Lieut. Edwin Houghton, 17th ME Regimental Order Book, Special Order #3, October 28, 1863, part 1, vol. 4 of 7.
72. Private Thomas Welch, Company G, who had been with the regiment for only two weeks, pled guilty to sleeping on duty on Oct. 29, 1864; Private John Harrington, Company G, was found asleep on Nov. 8, 1864; Private Horace Banks, Company E, pled guilty of sleeping on duty on Dec. 12, 1864; Private David Fields, Company F, pled guilty to leaving his post on Dec. 20, 1864; Private Alpheus Northrop, Company E, pled guilty of sleeping on duty on Jan. 10, 1865. All were tried in Jacksonville, in December and January 1865; some were found not guilty by lack of instruction, and others were fined. U.S. Army Courts-Martial, file MM 1797, National Archives.

At one trial, the judge advocate general asked if the accused was familiar with the Articles of War, which, the witness admitted, he likely was not. Court-martial of Private Thomas Welch, Company G, 17th Conn. Vols., Jan. 11, 1865, U.S. Army Courts-Martial, file MM 1797.

73. Col. Wm. H. Noble and H. Whitney Chatfield, 1st Lieut. and Post Adjutant,

Dec. 3, 1864, General Order 28, Book Records of Volunteer Union Organizations, 17th Conn. Regimental Order Book, Companies G to K.

74. Lieut. Col. A. H. Wilcoxson and George Peck 1st Lieut. and Acting Post Adjutant, Nov. 28, 1864, Special Orders 177, 17th Conn. Regimental Order Book, Company H.

75. Comstock diary, entry for Dec. 20, 1864, reprinted in Broun and Leech, *Roundsman of the Lord*, 54.

76. Lieut. Col. A. H. Wilcoxson and George Peck 1st Lieut. and Acting Post Adjutant, July 18, 1864, General Order 103, 17th Conn. Regimental Order Book, Company H.

77. Soldiers admitted to U.S. Christian Committee chaplains that they bought novels and other reading material from sutlers. Galwey, *Valiant Hours*, 71.

78. "Articles of War," 499, 506, 504, 512.

79. Foote, *Gentlemen and the Roughs*, 30–33.

80. Col. Wm. H. Noble and H. Whitney Chatfield, 1st Lieut. and Post Adjutant, Dec. 9, 1864, Special Orders no. 230, Book Records of Volunteer Union Organizations, 17th Conn. Regimental Order Book, Companies G to K.

81. Noble, "History of the 17th Regiment," 243–44.

82. Ibid., 248–49.

83. Gordon, *Broken Regiment*, 206–25.

84. Le Grand, *Military Handbook*, 25.

85. Diary of Lieut. Robert Taggart, 38th Penn. Infantry Regiment, entry for Apr. 29, 1862, Jay Luvaas Collection, folder 1.

86. Comstock, *Traps for the Young*, 21.

87. Ibid., 25, 136.

88. And the occasional woman. Ibid., 37–38.

89. Ibid., 37–38. Comstock also judged the ages of the youthful offenders as ranging from twelve to eighteen; ibid., 37.

90. Ibid., 27.

91. Ibid., 10.

92. Comstock diary, entry for Nov. 9, 1864, reprinted in Broun and Leech, *Roundsman of the Lord*, 56.

93. Ibid., entry for July 11, 1864, after p. 47.

94. Comstock, *Traps for the Young*, 10.

95. Ibid., 25.

96. Comstock diary, entry for Jan. 20, 1864, reprinted in Broun and Leech, *Roundsman of the Lord*, 45.

97. Trumbull, *Anthony Comstock, Fighter*, 36.

98. In the European context, this "Young Person" was often a naïve maiden, such as Georgina Podsnap, the Dickens character described above who narrowly avoids seduction. "'Podsnappery,'" a ridiculous combination of ignorance and self-righteousness, was "the target of merciless satire," according to Walter Kendrick. *Secret Museum*, 49.

99. Comstock, *Traps for the Young*, 6.
100. Trumbull, *Anthony Comstock, Fighter*, 20.
101. Ibid., 19–20.
102. Ibid., 21–22.

Chapter 4

1. Vorenberg, *Final Freedom*, 206–12.
2. Stanley, "Instead of Waiting," 732.
3. Michigan senator Jacob Howard, quoted in ibid., 743.
4. Ibid., 759.
5. Franke, "Becoming a Citizen," 255, 257.
6. "Postal Laws," *Congressional Globe*, 38th Cong., 2nd sess., no. 42, Feb. 8, 1865, 660–61.
7. Ibid., 661.
8. Ibid.
9. "Postal Laws," *Congressional Globe*, 38th Cong., 2nd sess., no. 61, Feb. 21, 1865, 965–66.
10. Information on senators' sons serving attained from the following: for Trumbull, Haines, "Walter Trumbull," *Yellowstone National Park*, https://www.nps.gov/parkhistory/online_books/haines1/iee4b.htm#trumbull (accessed March 26, 2016); for Dixon, "Commemorative Biographical Record of Hartford County, CT," part 1, 1–2; for Fessenden, Biographical Note, William Fessenden Collection; for Howard, Woodford, *Father Abraham's Children*, 94; for Ten Eyck, Biography, Tenodor Ten Eyck Papers; for Harris, Washington Post, *Civil War Stories*, n.p.; and for Cowan, Corporal James B. Cowan Enlistment, 54th Penn. Muster Out Roll, Civil War Muster Rolls and Related Records.
11. "Shameful," *Centinel of Freedom*, Newark, N.J., May 12, 1863, 4.
12. Register of Arrests for Offenses against the Postal Laws, 1:46.
13. "Minor Topics," *New York Times*, Feb. 15, 1868, 4.
14. Dennis, *Licentious Gotham*, 228.
15. "The Obscene Democracy," *New York Tribune*, Apr. 25, 1868, 4.
16. Mohr, *Abortion in America*, 212.
17. "Final Passage of the Bill for the Suppression of Indecent Literature," *New York Tribune*, 23 Apr. 1868, 9.
18. Ibid.
19. Ibid.
20. Mohr, *Abortion in America*, 200–205.
21. "An Act for the protection of the public against medical imposters and for the suppression of the crime of unlawful abortion," Mar. 20, 1867, *Proceedings and Acts of the General Assembly* 133:4551–56, and "An Act to repeal and re-enact the Act of 1867, Chapter one hundred and eighty-five, for the Suppression of the Crime of Unlawful Abortion," Mar. 30, 1868, *Proceedings and Acts of the General Assembly* 142:2652–54.

22. In the meantime, doctors emphatically made the case against abortion. Before the American Medical Association in 1864, Dr. Horatio Robinson Storer characterized native white reproduction as an imperative and pleaded with women "upon [whose] loins depends the future destiny of the nation." "All the fruitfulness of the present generation tasked to its utmost," Storer entreated, "can hardly fill the gaps in our population that have of late been made by disease and the sword, . . . while . . . the fertile savannas of the South, now disenthralled and first made habitable by freemen, offers homes for countless millions yet unborn. Shall they be filled by our own children or those of aliens?" (Storer, *Why Not?*, 85–86). American essayist Mary Abigail Dodge, writing under the pen name Gail Hamilton, countered in an 1868 pamphlet that defended women's rights, insisting that women should have children when they were prepared and educated to do so well (*Woman's Wrongs*, 182).

23. Mohr, *Abortion in America*, 206–10. The original measure threatened with up to a year in prison "any married woman being pregnant" who took "any drug, medicine or secret nostrum, for the purpose of producing an abortion or miscarriage." Debate regarding S.B. 285, Feb. 27, 1867, *Journal of the Senate of the State of Ohio*, 63:237. The law narrowly passed in the state, and the final version of it did not refer to married women but instead focused on the advertisement of abortion and birth control services, in particular drugs promising to produce abortion. "Punishment for publishing advertisements of secret drugs for use of females, etc., or selling, or giving such drug away, etc.," Apr. 16, 1867, *Statutes of the State of Ohio* chap. 1173, 1360–61.

24. "Marriage and Divorce," *New York Times*, Aug. 2, 1868, 4. See also "Divorce Made Easy," *New York Times*, Oct. 10, 1869, 4. Divorce remained exceedingly rare—fewer than two marriages in one thousand ended in divorce in 1870—but even this was higher than divorce rates found in Europe. Cott, *Public Vows*, 105–15.

25. Susan Pearson argues that these federal measures "made monogamy and legal marriage the single standard of family life in the United States" ("Birth of New Regulation," 430). Mormon women fiercely defended polygamy; at one protest meeting, Harriet Cook Young blamed monogamy for the problems of "adultery, prostitution, free-love" and abortion. Quoted in Cott, *Public Vows*, 112.

26. Pascoe, *What Comes Naturally*, 9.

27. "Obscene Books, Etc., Summary Report," Committee for the Suppression of Vice, Young Men's Christian Association, New York, Nov. 1872, Kautz Family YMCA Archives, box 1118, 7. The report is marked "PRIVATE AND CONFIDENTIAL."

28. Frank W. Ballard, "New York City as a Mission Field," Apr. 27, 1863, Kautz Family YMCA Archives, box 1118.

29. J. C. Thomas to Lt. Colonel Goddard, AAG, Aug. 1863, Joseph Conable Thomas Collection, 5; U.S. Christian Commission, 4th Annual Report, 1866, 88, Kautz Family YMCA Archives, box 2.

30. Minutes of the executive committee, U.S. Christian Commission, Jan. 27,

1865, Records of the U.S. Christian Commission, Entry 753, box 1; Ballard, "New York City as a Mission Field," 8.

31. Mohr, *Abortion in America*, 217.

32. Anthony Comstock to Hon. C. L. Merriam, House of Representatives, Jan. 18, 1873, quoted in "Obscene Literature," speech of Clinton L. Merriam before the House, Mar. 1, 1873, Kautz Family YMCA Archives, box 1118, 4–5.

33. Of these dead publishers of obscene materials, Comstock bragged "these [sic] are in their graves, and it is charged by their friends that I worried them to death. Be that as it may, I am sure that the world is better off without them." Comstock to Merriam, quoted in Merriam, "Obscene Literature," 5.

34. Broun and Leech, *Roundsman of the Lord*, 92.

35. Merriam, "Obscene Literature," 1.

36. Merriam and YMCA activists were likely encouraged in their efforts by a prohibition written into an omnibus Post Office Law passed in Congress on June 8, 1872, that, in order to protect federally employed mail carriers, prohibited "all liquids, poisons, glass, explosive materials, and obscene books" (sec. 133) and declared guilty of a misdemeanor any person who deposited in the mail "an obscene book, pamphlet, picture, print, or other publication of a vulgar or indecent character, or any letter upon the envelope of which, or postal card upon which scurrilous epithets may have been written or printed, or disloyal devices printed or engraved" (secs. 133 and 148), 42nd Cong., 2nd sess., 1872, chap. 335, 300–301, 303. "An Act to Revise, Consolidate, and Amend the Statutes Relating to the Post-Office Department," *Congressional Globe*, 42nd Cong., 2nd sess., 283–330.

37. The law was passed early in the morning on the last day of the session. Critics charged that Congress did not have the time to read the bill before voting on it. At the time, congressmen were preoccupied with the Crédit Mobilier scandal in which several members of Grant's administration were under suspicion for having taken bribes from the Union Pacific Railroad. Broun and Leech, *Roundsman of the Lord*, 128–44; Trumbull, *Anthony Comstock, Fighter*, 83–99.

38. Pearson, "Birth of New Regulation," 425. Pearson argues that the period 1865–1900 was notable not for marking the rise of laissez-faire; rather, in this period "statebuilders traversed the scales of government from the states to the federal government, and built a state based less on equal protection or individual rights than on police powers" (ibid., 424).

39. Although opposed to it, Woman's Christian Temperance Union women were less interested in combating birth control and abortion than alcohol consumption; whereas Comstock focused on arresting offenders, the union worked to prevent pornography from reaching children. Parker, *Purifying America*, 41, 9.

40. Bloom, "Stanhopes: Hidden Erotica of the 19th Century."

41. Comstock often complained about police inaction, for instance. Comstock to Merriam, quoted in Merriam, "Obscene Literature," 4.

42. Broun and Leech, *Roundsman of the Lord*, 156–57. Historian Linda Gordon has argued that, in arresting abortion providers, Comstock likely helped to com-

bat a serious public health hazard, as the abortion procedures and drugs available at the time were dangerous and often ended in complications or death. Gordon, *Woman's Body*, 50–52.

43. Comstock also claimed to have driven fifteen people to commit suicide. Van Doren, "Anthony Comstock," 331.

44. Comstock to Merriam, quoted in Merriam, "Obscene Literature," 5.

45. Broun and Leech, *Roundsman of the Lord*, 168.

46. Register of Arrests for Offenses against the Postal Laws, 2:289. Comstock wasn't the only one incensed with Grant's pardons in this case. A juror in the original case who suspected that the president had been given bad information about the case wrote a letter to the *New York Evening Post* indicating that the men—Byron Fox and Leander Fox—had even continued to circulate the "obscene" items while in jail awaiting trial. A. Juror, "The Pardon of the Foxes," *New York Evening Post*, Apr. 3, 1874, 4.

47. Comstock diary, entry for Nov. 26, 1873, reprinted in, Broun and Leech, *Roundsman of the Lord*, 168.

48. Among his ruses, Comstock often posed as a married woman seeking birth control advice or drugs promising to induce abortion.

49. Foner, *Reconstruction*, 504–5.

50. Tone, *Devices and Desires*, 40–41.

51. Craig LeMay found the first appearance of the term "Comstockery" in an editorial in the *New York Times* in 1895 criticizing Comstock's raid on a French bookstore in the name of "protecting the morals of the young and inexperienced" (quoted in LeMay, "America's Censor," 30). See also *American Heritage Dictionary of the English Language*, 5th ed., s.v. "Comstockery," http://www.thefreedictionary.com/Comstockery (accessed, July 27 2015); and *Farlex Free Dictionary*, s.v. "Comstockery, http://www.thefreedictionary.com/Comstockery (accessed July 27, 2015).

52. Broun and Leech, *Roundsman of the Lord*, 235.

53. Pisanus Fraxi, *Index Librorum*, xxxi.

54. Stoops, "Class and Gender Dynamics," 141–43.

55. Chauncey, *Gay New York*, 34, 101, 146–49, 155–57.

Epilogue

1. Hawley, "American Publishers," 478.
2. Blanchard, *Art of Real Pleasure*, 7.
3. Ibid., 11.
4. Faust, "'We Should Grow Too Fond of It,'" 380.
5. Ibid., 382.
6. Marcus, *Other Victorians*, 267–68.
7. Ibid., 271.
8. Ibid., 274.
9. Ibid., 276.

10. Ibid., 279.
11. Guelzo, *Last Invasion*, 3–4.
12. Ibid., 104.
13. Ibid., 209. Colonel Martin Hardin quoted in ibid., 124 (note 19, 514).
14. Carl Schurz quoted in ibid., 366–67.
15. Ibid., 444.
16. Ibid., 444–45.
17. "2014 Gilder Lehrman Lincoln Prize," News@Gettysburg, http://www.gettysburg.edu/news_events/press_release_detail.dot?id=95c494ec-2e78-4c9c-a05f-c9da1ca14909 (accessed March 26, 2016).
18. Lyman Tower Sargent locates Blanchard's writing in a tradition of utopian literature focusing on "sexual activity in a context of gender equality"; in his thoughts about society, politics, and sex, Blanchard was close to French philosopher Charles Fourier, whose works about which Blanchard was likely familiar. Sargent, "Calvin Blanchard," 314.

BIBLIOGRAPHY

―――――♦―――――

PRIMARY SOURCES

Manuscript Collections

Bloomington, Ind.
    Kinsey Institute for Research in Sex, Gender, and Reproduction, Indiana University
Brunswick, Maine
    William Fessenden Collection, George J. Mitchell Department of Special Collections and Archives, Bowdoin College Library; available at https://library.bowdoin.edu/arch/mss/wpfg.shtml
Carlisle, Pa.
    Civil War Document Collection, U.S. Army Heritage and Education Center
    Jay Luvaas Collection, U.S. Army Heritage and Education Center
Harrisburg, Pa.
    54th Pennsylvania Muster Out Roll, Civil War Muster Rolls and Related Records, 1861–66, Records of the Department of Military and Veterans Affairs, RG 19, series 19.11, Pennsylvania Historical and Museum Commission; available through Ancestry.com
    William Neel Collection, Pennsylvania Historical and Museum Collection
New York, N.Y.
    District Attorney's Indictment Papers, 1861–70, New York City Municipal Archives
Philadelphia, Pa.
    Philadelphia Civil War and Underground Railroad Museum Collections, The Heritage Center of the Union League of Philadelphia
    Van Pelt Library, University of Pennsylvania
St. Paul, Minn.
    Kautz Family YMCA Archives, Andersen Library, University of Minnesota

Tucson, Ariz.
   Tenodor Ten Eyck Papers, Special Collections, University of Arizona; available at http://speccoll.library.arizona.edu/collections/tenodor-ten-eyck-papers
Washington, D.C.
   Library of Congress
      Joseph Conable Thomas Collection
      Prints and Photographs Division
   National Archives
      Records of the U.S. Christian Commission, RG 94
      Regimental order books, RG 94
      Register of Arrests for Offenses against the Postal Laws, 1864–97, Records of the Post Office Department, Bureau of Chief Inspector, 2 vols., RG 28
      U.S. Army Courts-Martial
Worcester, Mass.
   American Broadsides and Ephemera, American Antiquarian Society

Periodicals

Centinel of Freedom
Christian Recorder
Columbian Register (New Haven, Conn.)
Frank Leslie's
Harper's New Monthly Magazine
Liberator
National Era (Washington, D.C.)
New York Daily Tribune
New York Evening Post
New York Herald
New York Times
New York Tribune
Philadelphia Inquirer
United States Service Magazine

Published Works

Alcott, William. *Familiar Letters to Young Men on Various Subjects*. Buffalo, N.Y., 1850.

———. *The Young Men's Guide*. Boston: T. R. Marvin, 1849.

Anonymous. *The Murdered Queen! Or, Caroline of Brunswick, a Diary of the Court of George IV, by a Lady of Rank*. London: W. Emans, 1838.

"Articles of War." In *Revised Regulations for the Army of the United States, 1861*, 499–516. Philadelphia: Lippincott, 1861.

Baker, Colonel Lafayette. *A History of the United States Secret Service*. Philadelphia: King and Baird, 1867.

Beecher, Henry Ward. *Lectures to Young Men on Various Important Subjects* (1846). New York: John B. Alden, 1890.

Blanchard, Calvin. *The Art of Real Pleasure* (1864). New York: Arno Press and New York Times, 1971.

Bowen, James L. *Massachusetts in the War, 1861–1865*. Springfield, Mass.: Clark W. Bryan, 1889.

Brainerd, Cephas. *Christian Work in the Army prior to the Organization of the United States Christian Commission*. New York: John Medole, 1866.
Brewster, Charles Harvey. *When This Cruel War Is Over: The Civil War Letters of Charles Harvey Brewster*. Edited by David Blight. Boston: University of Massachusetts Press, 1992.
Clay, E. W. "Amalgamation Series." New York: John Childs, 1839.
"Commemorative Biographical Record of Hartford County, Conn." 2 vols. Chicago, Ill.: J. H. Beers, 1901.
Comstock, Anthony. *Traps for the Young*. Edited by J. M. Buckley, D.D. New York: Funk and Wagnalls, 1883.
Congressional Globe: The Official Proceedings of Congress, 38th Congress, 2nd sess. Washington, D.C.: Library of Congress. Available at https://memory.loc.gov/ammem/amlaw/lwcglink.html.
De Forest, John William. "Sheridan's Battle of Winchester." *Harper's New Monthly Magazine* 30, no. 176 (January 1865): 195–200.
——— . *A Volunteer's Adventures: A Union Captain's Record of the Civil War*. Edited by James Croushore. New Haven, Conn.: Yale University Press, 1946.
Dickens, Charles. *Our Mutual Friend*. London: Chapman and Hall, 1864–65.
"The Ethics and Humanities of War." *United States Service Magazine*, vol. 1, no. 2, February 1864, 113–25.
Fryer, D. F., Sergeant, Co. D. *History of the Eightieth Ohio Veteran Volunteer Infantry from 1861–1865*. Newcomerstown, Ohio, 1904.
Galwey, Thomas Frank. *The Valiant Hours: Narrative of "Captain Brevet," an Irish-American in the Army of the Potomac*. Harrisburg, Pa.: Stackpole Books, 1961.
Garrison, William Lloyd. "Address to the Colonization Society" (July 4, 1829). Available at http://teachingamericanhistory.org/library/document/address-to-the-colonization-society/.
Graham, James, Second Lieutenant. "'Had a Pleasant Time': Excerpts from the Diary of a Yankee in Dixie." Edited by Albert Castel. *Blue & Gray Magazine*, March 1986, 32–37.
Graham, Sylvester. *A Lecture to Young Men, On Chastity*. 4th ed. Boston: George W. Light, 1 Cornhill, 1838.
Hamilton, Gail [Mary Abigail Dodge]. *Woman's Wrongs: A Counter-Irritant*. Boston: Ticknor and Fields, 1868.
Helper, Hinton Rowan. *The Impending Crisis of the South: How to Meet It*. New York: Burdick Brothers, 1857.
Higginson, Thomas Wentworth. *Army Life in a Black Regiment*. Boston: Fields, Osgood, 1870.
Ibson, John. *Picturing Men: A Century of Male Relationships in Everyday American Photography*. Chicago: University of Chicago Press, 2006.
Journal of the Senate of the State of Ohio. Hathi Trust. Available at http://catalog.hathitrust.org/Record/012323116.

Le Grand, Louis, M.D. *The Military Handbook, and Soldier's Manual of Information.* New York: Beadle, 1861.

Marcus, Edward, ed. *A New Canaan Private in the Civil War: Letters of Justus M. Silliman, 17th Connecticut Volunteers.* New Canaan, Conn.: New Canaan Historical Society, 1984.

"Misery vs. Muscle." *Frank Leslie's Illustrated,* 221, no. 9, February 25, 1860, 192.

Noble, William H. "History of the Seventeenth Connecticut." *The History of Fairfield County, Connecticut.* Edited by D. Hamilton Hurd. Philadelphia, Pa.: J. W. Lewis & Co, 1888.

———. "History of the 17th Regiment Connecticut Volunteer Infantry." In *Ye Historie of Ye Town of Greenwich, County of Fairfield and State of Connecticut,* edited by Spencer Percival Mead, 243–58. New York: Knickerbocker Press, 1911.

Patrick, Marsena Rudolph. *Inside Lincoln's Army: The Diary of Marsena Rudolph Patrick, Provost Marshal General, Army of the Potomac.* Edited by David S. Sparks. New York: Thomas Yoseloff, 1964.

Pisanus Fraxi [Henry Spencer Ashbee]. *Index Librorum Prohibitorum being Notes Bio, Biblio, Econo graphical and Critical on Curious and Uncommon Books.* London: privately printed, 1877.

Proceedings and Acts of the General Assembly (of Maryland). Archives of Maryland Online. Available at http://aomol.msa.maryland.gov.

Seventeenth Connecticut Volunteers at Gettysburg, June 30th, and July 1st, 2d and 3d, 1884. Bridgeport, Conn.: Standard Association, 1884.

Statutes of the State of Ohio in Continuation of Curwen's Statutes at Large . . . Cincinnati: Robert Clarke, 1876.

Storer, Horatio Robinson, M.D. *Why Not? A Book for Every Woman.* American Medical Association Prize Essay, [1864]. Boston: Lee and Shepard, 1866. Available at Kinsey Institute Special Collections.

Stowe, Harriet Beecher. *Uncle Tom's Cabin.* London: John Cassell, Ludgate Hall, 1852.

Thompson, George [a.k.a. Greenhorn]. *City Crimes; or, Life in New York and Boston.* Boston: William and Berry, 1849.

Weld, Theodore Dwight. *American Slavery as It Is: Testimony of a Thousand Witnesses.* New York: American Anti-Slavery Society, 1839.

SECONDARY SOURCES

Adelman, Gary. "The Third Battle of Winchester." *Hallowed Ground Magazine,* Winter 2004. http://www.civilwar.org/battlefields/thirdwinchester/third-winchester-history-articles/winchesteradelman.html.

Barber, E. Susan, and Charles F. Ritter. "'Physical Abuse . . . and Rough Handling': Race, Gender, and Sexual Justice in the Occupied South." In *Occupied Women: Gender, Military Occupation, and the American Civil War,* edited by Lee Ann

Whites and Alecia Long, 49–66. Baton Rouge: Louisiana State University Press, 2009.

Bederman, Gail. *Manliness and Civilization: A Cultural History of Gender and Race in the United States, 1880–1917.* Chicago: University of Chicago Press, 1996.

Bentley, Paul. "'Mummy Porn' Fifty Shades of Grey Outstrips Harry Potter to Become Fastest Selling Paperback of All Time." *Daily Mail* (London), June 17, 2012. http://www.dailymail.co.uk/news/article-2160862/Fifty-Shades-Of-Grey-book-outstrips-Harry-Potter-fastest-selling-paperback-time.html.

Berends, Kurt O. "'Wholesome Reading Purifies and Elevates the Man': The Religious Military Press in the Confederacy." In *Religion and the American Civil War*, edited by Randall M. Miller, Harry S. Stout, and Charles Reagan Wilson, 131–66. New York: Oxford University Press, 1988.

Bloom, Matt. "Stanhopes: Hidden Erotica of the 19th Century." *Kinsey Institute Newsletter* 18, no. 2. http://www.kinseyinstitute.org/newsletter/sp2014/stanhopes.html.

Broun, Heywood, and Margaret Leech. *Anthony Comstock: Roundsman of the Lord.* New York: Albert and Charles, 1927.

Bushman, Richard Lyman. *The Refinement of America: Persons, Houses, Cities.* New York: Vintage, 1993.

Chauncey, George. *Gay New York: Gender, Urban Culture, and the Making of a Gay Male World, 1890–1940.* New York: Basic Books, 1994.

Clinton, Catherine. "'Public Women' and Sexual Politics during the American Civil War." In *Battle Scars: Gender and Sexuality in the American Civil War*, edited by Catherine Clinton and Nina Silber, 61–77. New York: Oxford University Press, 2006.

Cohen, Patricia Cline. *The Murder of Helen Jewett.* New York: Vintage, 1999.

Cott, Nancy F. *Public Vows: A History of Marriage and the Nation.* Cambridge, Mass.: Harvard University Press, 2000.

Das, Santanu. *Touch and Intimacy in First World War Literature.* Cambridge: Cambridge University Press, 2005.

Dennis, Kelly. *Art/Porn: A History of Seeing and Touching.* New York: Oxford, 2009.

Dennis, Donna. *Licentious Gotham: Erotic Publishing and Its Prosecution in Nineteenth-Century New York.* Cambridge, Mass.: Harvard University Press, 2009.

Erikson, Paul Joseph. "Welcome to Sodom: The Cultural Work of City-Mysteries Fiction in Antebellum America." Ph.D. diss., University of Texas at Austin, 2005.

Faust, Drew Gilpin. "'We Should Grow Too Fond of It': Why We Love the Civil War." *Civil War History* 50, no. 4 (2004): 368–83.

Foner, Eric. *Reconstruction: America's Unfinished Revolution, 1863–1877.* New York: Harper and Row, 1988.

Foote, Lorien. *The Gentlemen and the Roughs: Violence, Honor, and Manhood in the Union Army.* New York: New York University Press, 2010.

Franke, Katherine. "Becoming a Citizen: Reconstruction Era Regulation of African American Marriages." *Yale Journal of Law and Humanities* 11 (1999): 251–309.
Fussell, Paul. *The Great War and Modern Memory*. New York: Oxford University Press, 1976.
Gallman, J. Matthew. "Snapshots: Images of Men in the United States Colored Troops." *American Nineteenth Century History* 13, no. 2 (2012): 127–51.
Glatthaar, Joseph. "A Tale of Two Armies: The Confederate Army of Northern Virginia and the Union Army of the Potomac." Fifty-Fourth Annual Robert Fortenbaugh Memorial Lecture, November 19, 2015. *Journal of the Civil War Era* (September 2016).
Goddu, Teresa A. *Gothic America: Narrative, History, and Nation*. New York: Cambridge University Press, 1997.
Gordon, Lesley. *A Broken Regiment: The 16th Connecticut's Civil War*. Baton Rouge: Louisiana State University Press, 2014.
Gordon, Linda. *Woman's Body, Woman's Right: Birth Control in America*. New York: Penguin, 1990.
Graham, Thomas. "The Home Front: Civil War Times in St. Augustine." In *Civil War Times in St. Augustine*, edited by Jacqueline K. Fretwell, 19–45. Port Salerno, Fla.: St. Augustine Historical Society, 1988.
Greenberg, Amy. *Manifest Manhood and the Antebellum American Empire*. New York: Cambridge University Press, 2005.
Guelzo, Allen. *Gettysburg: The Last Invasion*. New York: Knopf, 2013.
Halttunen, Karen. "Humanitarianism and the Pornography of Pain in Anglo American Culture." *American Historical Review* 100, no. 2 (1995): 303–34.
Haines, Aubrey L. *Yellowstone National Park: Its Exploration and Establishment*. U.S. Department of the Interior, National Park Service, Washington, 1974. https://www.nps.gov/parkhistory/online_books/haines1/iee4b.htm#trumbull (accessed March 26, 2016).
Hawley, Elizabeth Haven. "American Publishers of Indecent Books, 1840–1890." Ph.D. diss., Georgia Institute of Technology, 2005.
Herzog, Dagmar. *Sex after Fascism: Memory and Morality in Twentieth-Century Germany*. Princeton, N.J.: Princeton University Press, 2007.
Higonnet, Margaret Randolph, Jane Jenson, Sonya Michel, and Margaret Collins Weitz, eds. *Behind the Lines: Gender and the Two World Wars*. New Haven, Conn.: Yale University Press, 1987.
Hijiya, James. *J. W. De Forest and the Rise of American Gentility*. Boston: University Press of New England, 1988.
Horowitz, Helen Lefkowitz. *Rereading Sex: Battles over Sexual Knowledge and Suppression in Nineteenth-Century America*. New York: Knopf, 2002.
Hunt, Lynn. *The Invention of Pornography: Obscenity and the Origins of Modernity, 1500–1800*. New York: Zone Books, 1996.
Hunt, Roger D. *Colonels in Blue — Union Army Colonels of the Civil War: The New England States*. Atglen, Pa.: Schiffer, 2011.

Jeffords, Susan. *The Remasculinization of America: Gender and the Vietnam War.* Bloomington: Indiana University Press, 1989.

Johnson, Susan. *Roaring Camp: The Social World of the California Gold Rush.* New York: Norton, 2000.

Kendrick, Walter. *The Secret Museum: Pornography in Modern Culture.* Berkeley: University of California Press, 1997.

Legal Information Institute. "Obscenity." Cornell University Law School. https://www.law.cornell.edu/wex/obscenity (accessed June 28, 2015).

LeMay, Craig. "America's Censor: Anthony Comstock and Free Speech." *Communications and the Law* 19, no. 1 (1997): 1–59.

Leonard, Elizabeth. *All the Daring of the Soldier: Women of the Civil War Armies.* New York: Penguin Books, 2001.

Linderman, Gerald. *Embattled Courage: The Experience of Combat in the American Civil War.* New York: Free Press, 1989.

Lowry, Thomas P. *The Story the Soldiers Wouldn't Tell: Sex in the Civil War.* Mechanicsburg, Pa.: Stackpole Books, 1994.

Marcus, Steven. *The Other Victorians: A Study of Sexuality and Pornography in Mid-Nineteenth Century England.* New York: Basic Books, 1964.

Massey, Mary Elizabeth. "The Effects of Shortages on the Confederate Homefront." *Arkansas Historical Quarterly* 9, no. 3 (1950): 172–93.

McPherson, James M. *Battle Cry of Freedom: The Civil War Era.* New York: Oxford University Press, 1988.

———. *For Cause and Comrades: Why Men Fought in the Civil War.* New York: Oxford University Press, 1997.

Mitchell, Reid. *The Vacant Chair: The Northern Soldier Leaves Home.* New York: Oxford University Press, 1993.

Mohr, James C. *Abortion in America: The Origins and Evolution of National Policy.* New York: Oxford University Press, 1979.

Musick, Michael. "Spirited and Spicy Scenes?" *Civil War Times Illustrated*, January 1973, 26–29.

News at Gettysburg. "2015 Gilder Lehrman Lincoln Prize Awarded to Allen Guelzo and Martin Johnson." http://www.gettysburg.edu/news_events/press_release_detail.dot?id=95c494ec-2e78-4c9c-a05f-c9da1ca14909. Accessed March 26, 2016.

Parker, Alison M. *Purifying America: Women, Cultural Reform, and Pro-Censorship Activism, 1873–1933.* Urbana: University of Illinois Press, 1997.

Pascoe, Peggy. *What Comes Naturally: Miscegenation Law and the Making of Race in America.* New York: Oxford University Press, 2009.

Paul, James C. N., and Murray L. Schwartz. *Federal Censorship: Obscenity in the Mail.* Westport, Conn.: Greenwood Press, 1961.

Pearson, Susan. "A Birth of New Regulation: The State of the State after the Civil War." *Journal of the Civil War Era* 5, no. 3 (2015): 422–39.

Sargent, Lyman Tower. "Calvin Blanchard and *The Art of Real Pleasure*." *Utopian Studies* 24, no. 2 (2013): 312–28.
Schweiger, Beth Barton. "The Literate South: Reading before Emancipation." *Journal of the Civil War Era* 3, no. 3 (2013): 331–59.
Silber, Nina. *The Romance of Reunion: Northerners and the South, 1865–1900*. Chapel Hill: University of North Carolina Press, 1997.
Stanley, Amy Dru. "Instead of Waiting for the Thirteenth Amendment: The War Power, Slave Marriage, and Inviolate Human Rights." *American Historical Review* 115 (June 2010): 732–65.
Stewart, David M. "Cultural Work, City Crime, Reading, Pleasure." *American Literary History* 9, no. 4 (1997): 676–701.
Stoops, Jamie. "Class and Gender Dynamics of the Pornography Trade in Late Nineteenth Century Britain." *Historical Journal* 58, no. 1 (2015): 137–56.
Stott, Richard. *Jolly Fellows: Male Milieus in Nineteenth-Century America*. Baltimore, Md.: Johns Hopkins University Press, 2009.
Tone, Andrea. *Devices and Desires: A History of Contraceptives in America*. New York: Hill and Wang, 2001.
Trumbull, Charles Gallaudet. *Anthony Comstock, Fighter*. 2nd ed. New York: Fleming H. Revell, 1913.
Van Doren, Mark. "Anthony Comstock." In *Dictionary of American Biography*, 330–31. New York: Charles Scribner, 1930.
Vorenberg, Michael. *Final Freedom: The Civil War, the Abolition of Slavery, and the Thirteenth Amendment*. New York: Cambridge University Press, 2004.
Walters, Ronald. "The Erotic South: Civilization and Sexuality in American Abolitionism." *American Quarterly* 25, no. 2 (1973): 177–201.
Washington Post. *Civil War Stories: A 150th Anniversary Collection*, Washington, D.C.: Diversion Books, 2013.
Whites, Lee Ann. "The Civil War as a Crisis in Gender." In *Divided Houses: Gender and the Civil War*, edited by Catherine Clinton and Nina Silber, 3–21. New York: Oxford University Press, 1992.
———. "Crisis in Masculinity: Civil War History as a View from Somewhere." In *The Civil War as a Crisis in Gender: August, Georgia, 1860–1890*, 1–14. Athens: University of Georgia Press, 1999.
Woodford, Frank B. *Father Abraham's Children: Michigan Episodes in the Civil War*. Detroit, Mich.: Wayne State University Press, 1961.
Woodworth, Steven E. *While God Is Marching On: The Religious World of Civil War Soldiers*. Lawrence: University Press of Kansas, 2001.
Yacovone, Donald. "'Surpassing the Love of Women': Victorian Manhood and the Language of Fraternal Love." In *A Shared Experience: Men, Women, and the History of Gender*, edited by Laura McCall and Donald Yacovone, 195–221. New York: New York University Press, 1998.

INDEX

Abolitionists, 3, 14, 27–29; and congressional gag rule, 88
Abortion, 2, 10, 89, 90, 94, 102; abortion providers, 4, 122–23 (n. 42)
Ackerman, George, 17, 22–23, 33, 93
Alcott, William, 64–65
Amalgamation, 29–31, 30 (ill.)
Antebellum erotic imagination, 10, 30–31, 30 (ill.), 41
Antiabortion laws, 3, 6, 7, 89–91, 97, 98, 121 (n. 22)
Antipornography law: Senate Bill 390 (1865), 1, 10, 31, 84–87, 90, 104; Comstock Law (1873), 10, 92, 95, 99–100, 105; in Maryland, 88, 90, 92; in New York, 88–89, 92
Ashbee, Herbert Spencer, 12, 19, 100
Atchison, John, 14–15, 17, 19, 31, 33

Baker, Col. Lafayette, 26–27, 29, 31
Ballard, Frank, 91–92, 93
Beecher, Henry Ward, 45
Birth control, 3, 4, 5, 10, 90–91, 94, 102; anti–birth control laws, 7, 96–97, 98
Blair, Montgomery, 26
Blanchard, Calvin, 104–8
British antipornography, 100–102; and Lord Campbell's Obscene Publications Act, 12, 13, 99

Cartes de visite, 8, 23, 43–49, 44 (ill.), 52, 57, 63
Censorship, 4, 110 (n. 15). *See also* Comstock, Anthony
Cicily Martin, 37, 38, 39 (ill.), 40
Circulars, 19, 20–21 (ill.), 22, 25–26, 31, 33, 41, 42, 93; and catalogs, 25, 93
Collamer, Jacob, 1, 12, 85, 86
Comstock, Anthony, 2, 3, 9, 10, 13, 26, 52, 84, 99 (ill.), 104, 108; and antisodomy, 102–3; "Comstockery," 98–99, 123 (n. 51); as Pvt. Comstock in the U.S. Army, 60–71, 74–77, 79–81; as special agent to the U.S. Post Office, 96–97; and *Traps for the Young*, 77–79; and the YMCA's antipornography campaign, 92–99;
Comstock, Sgt. Samuel, 59–61, 69, 77
Condoms, 100
Confederates, 42, 66, 71, 73, 109 (n. 1), 110–11 (n. 27)
Customs laws, 12–13

Day, Benjamin Henry, 2, 87
De Forest, Capt. John W., 71
Democratic Party, 86, 88
Dickens, Charles, 63
Doctors, 90–91, 101, 121 (n. 22)
Domesticity, 37, 56–57, 58

Emancipation, 6, 82–84, 90; Emancipation Proclamation, 82

Fanny Hill, or Memoirs of a Woman of Pleasure, 11, 14, 17, 20 (ill.), 22, 33–40, 35 (ill.), 72
Farrell, John, 15–17
Faust, Drew G., 8, 105–6
Flagellation, 27–29, 33, 37
Flash press, 17
Frank Leslie's, 24 (ill.), 42, 55
Freedmen's Bureau, 83, 86
Free love, 4, 98
Fugitive Slave Law (1850), 29

Galwey, Thomas, 51–52
Garnet, Henry Highland, 82
Garrison, William Lloyd, 29
Gender, 5, 6, 7, 8, 91, 94, 108. *See also* Domesticity; Manliness, manhood
Gettysburg, Battle of, 59, 69, 76–77, 106–8
Godey's Lady's Book, 50–51 (ill.)
Graham, James, 71–73, 101
Grant, Ulysses S., 1, 71, 73, 97–98, 122 (n. 37)
Grimke, Angelina, 30–31

Harper's Weekly, 42
Hayes, Rutherford B., 98
Higginson, Thomas Wentworth, 48
Homosexuality, 4, 7, 102–3
Hunt, Lynn, 27, 36, 62–63

Jewett, Helen, 42, 43, 87
Johnson, Reverdy, 86, 88, 109 (n. 4)

Lincoln, Abraham, 26–27, 41, 42
Lyman, 2nd Lt. William, 42–45, 49–50, 52–53

Manliness, manhood, 6, 7, 8, 10, 49, 61, 64, 66, 69–71, 73, 94, 101

Marriage, 11, 70, 83–84, 86, 90, 98–99, 101; marital crisis, 90–91
Masturbation, 7, 37, 65
Mayo, Thomas, 36
McFarland, Pvt. William, 34, 38
Merrimam, Clinton L., 93–94, 98, 99–100

Noble, Col. William, 67, 74–77
Noms de plume, 16, 18 (ill.), 22, 25

Ormsby, Thomas, 14–15, 17, 19–22, 33; Thomas Ormsby's Commission Bureau, 19, 21 (ill.)

Patrick, Marsena Rudolph, 25
Paul de Kock, 16, 18 (ill.), 22, 29, 54
Peirce, Ebenezer, 33–40, 45, 49, 57–58, 72, 101
Phelps, Maj. Lorenzo, 53
Photography, 6, 10, 25, 46–47, 55, 88, 105
Playing cards, 8, 57, 71, 94
Podsnappery, 63, 99, 119 (n. 98)
Police, 14, 16, 22, 89, 92, 95–96, 102
Pornotopia 106–8
Postmaster, 22, 86, 87, 109 (n. 1)
Pranks, 71, 75
Prisoners of war, 42, 76, 79, 104
Prostitution, prostitutes, 3, 5, 7, 13, 26, 28, 33–36, 42, 46, 73, 89, 90; brothel guides, 22; harems, 28

Rape, 50
Regina v. Hicklin, 63
Republican Party, 3, 89
Restell, Madame, 96–97
Roe v. Wade, 3

Seventeenth Connecticut, Volunteer Infantry, 59–61, 64, 66–71, 74–77, 79, 92; monument to, 60 (ill.), 79–80
Sexual culture, 5, 9, 36, 37, 53–54, 57–58
Sherman, John, 85–86

Index

Sherman, William Tecumseh, 1, 85
Silliman, Justis, 59–60, 66–67, 68–69
Slavery, 14, 27–29, 41, 83–84, 108, 112 (n. 44)
Stanhopes, 95, 96 (ill.), 97 (ill.)
Stereographs, stereoscope, 8, 23, 55 (ill.), 56 (ill.), 55–56, 58, 88, 93, 94
Stowe, Harriet Beecher, 27–28, 112 (n. 44)

Thirteenth Amendment, 82–84
Thompson, George, 16–17, 18 (ill.), 29
Tousley, Capt. M. G., 25–26, 31, 41, 49, 52
Traps for the Young, 31, 77–79, 78 (ill.)
Trumbull, Charles Gallaudet, 70, 81
Trumbull, Lyman, 87

U.S. Army courts-martial, 10, 33–58, 74
U.S. Christian Commission, 4, 23–24, 92
U.S. Congress, 1, 4, 23, 27, 94–95, 99–100; 38th, 82–87; 42nd, 93–95, 98

U.S. mail, 1, 2, 4, 10, 17, 22, 26, 85–87, 92, 110 (n. 15)

Vampires, 26, 28–29, 31
Venus Miscellany, 17, 22, 93
Violence, 8, 10, 14, 28, 37, 42, 49, 57, 59, 62, 78, 102, 104–8
Voyeurism, peeping, 28, 36, 38, 43, 54, 55

Waldron, Capt. Hampden, 53–54
Webster, Daniel, 29
Weld, Theodore D., 27–30
Woman's Christian Temperance Union, 95
Wood, Fernando, 15–17

Young Men's Christian Association (YMCA), 3, 4, 88, 91–92, 102–3; Army Committee of, 4; Committee for the Suppression of Vice, 92–93
"Young person," 5, 10, 26, 63, 80, 90, 97, 102; youth, 12, 14, 31, 108

www.ingramcontent.com/pod-product-compliance
Lightning Source LLC
Chambersburg PA
CBHW020853160426
43192CB00007B/912